Behind the Scenes at The British Museum

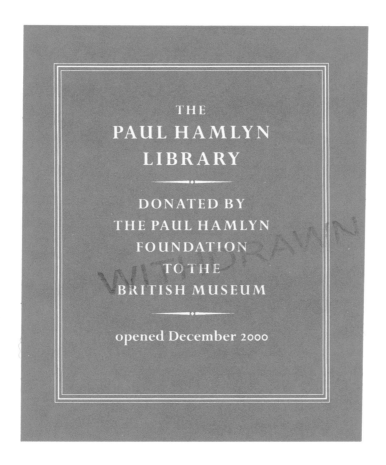

CRACKING CODES
THE ROSETTA STONE AND DECIPHERMENT

An exhibition to celebrate
the 200th anniversary of the
discovery of the Rosetta Stone
the key to the decipherment of
Ancient Egyptian hieroglyphs

Behind the Scenes at
The British Museum

Edited by
Andrew Burnett and John Reeve

THE BRITISH MUSEUM PRESS

© 2001 The Trustees of The British Museum

First published in 2001 by The British Museum Press
A division of The British Museum Company Ltd
46 Bloomsbury Street, London WC1B 3QQ

A catalogue record for this book is available from the British Library

ISBN 0 7141 2196 7

Cover photograph by Dudley Hubbard, © The British Museum
Photography by The British Museum Photography and Imaging,
© The British Museum, except where indicated
Designed and typeset in Photina, Frutiger and Bliss by Martin Richards
Printed in Slovenia by Korotan

Cover Conservation of Roman
marble sculpture.

Frontispiece Moving the Rosetta
Stone for the *Cracking Codes*
exhibition.

CONTENTS

ACKNOWLEDGEMENTS

This book has nothing to do with Kate Atkinson's well-known novel under a superficially similar title – this one really is about life in a museum. In fact, it owes more in its conception to Geoff Ryman's 253, though our account is not fictional and does not end in disaster! But by allowing the people in The British Museum to speak for themselves, we hope we have been able to bring out the diversity of background, style and approach that characterizes our colleagues and their work. To them we owe the greatest debt, for being ready to reveal themselves in a way that has not been tried before. In doing so, we hope they have helped to bridge the gap between the generalized remarks found in official reports or books about museology and what the public actually sees.

As well as the contributors several people have been extremely helpful, not to mention tolerant: Clio Whittaker, Nina Shandloff and Antonia Brook for their work on the manuscript, Martin Richards for the design, Dudley Hubbard for the cover photograph, Richard Parkinson for the frontispiece and Christopher Date for much help with the illustrations and for advice generally. Most of the photographs, except where otherwise acknowledged, were taken by members of the Museum's photographic department. We are grateful for permission to reprint passages published elsewhere by Ian Stead, Don Brothwell and Nigel Williams. We also thank Robert Anderson and Carol Homden for reading a version of the text and pointing out some errors. But we cheerfully shoulder responsibility for all that follows.

Andrew Burnett
John Reeve

The purpose of The British Museum has remained remarkably constant, even though both the Museum and its contents have changed a great deal since its foundation in 1753. The original *Fundamental principles from which the Trustees do not think they can in honor or conscience depart* envisaged that the collection should be preserved intact and 'kept for the use and benefit of the publick, who may have free access to view and peruse the same'. A Royal Commission of 1849 examined how the Museum might be made 'most effective for the advancement of Literature, Science and the Arts'. Similar formulations are still in use: 'the British Museum exists to promote knowledge of the history of civilization' (1996), or, as the most recent corporate identity proclaims, its role is one of 'illuminating world cultures'.

Preservation, education and enjoyment have thus always been important, although the emphasis has changed from time to time. In the nineteenth century, the noise generated by 'babes in arms' caused their entry to be prohibited until 1879. And, despite the assertion during the same period that 'the duty of the Trustees is carefully to preserve and efficiently to exhibit the objects entrusted to them ... they are not in any other sense connected with education', changes in the definition of education meant that the creation of an education service in the Museum in 1970

Although free, entry to the Museum was by ticket until the early 19th century.

No² This Ticket entitles

to a Sight of the

BRITISH MUSEUM,

at the Hour of *One* on *Wednesday*
the *3* of *March* 1790.

No Money is to be given to the Servants.

A queue for the Tutankhamun exhibition in 1972.

was not so much a novel departure as an extension of something that was already happening, in a new climate where education had moved out of the classroom.

Within this overall framework, what actually takes place in the Museum has been the product of internal development and external influences. The most obvious changes concern what is or is not included in its collection. The British Museum was originally conceived as a universal collection, but the establishment of new institutions has put much elsewhere. Oil paintings were transferred to the National Gallery in 1824 and the National Portrait Gallery in 1870, although an enormous collection of art remains, both Western drawings and prints and non-Western art in all media. A huge number of natural history specimens were moved to the separate Natural History Museum between 1880 and 1883. The world's greatest library was formally devolved to a new institution in 1973, and the books and manuscripts actually left for the new British Library building in 1998.

If these changes have altered the Museum, they have not discouraged the visitor. The Museum first opened to the public on 15 January 1759. At first, visitors were admitted by ticket and shown round in groups of five or ten. By 1810, visitor numbers had risen to what was regarded as an alarming 120 a day! But even that figure was sometimes surpassed. On Easter Monday 1837, the first time that the Museum opened on a public holiday, 23,895 people came. In 1851, the year of the Great Exhibition, visitors numbered an astonishing 2,527,216. Although that figure was exceptional, there has been a steady growth in visitors, from more than a million a year in 1923 to regularly more than five million. The most recent building developments at the Museum – the Great Court and the Study Centre – are only the latest response in a continuing effort to provide appropriate facilities for an enormous number of people whose expectations of the Museum are greater all the time.

Nowadays the visitor is the most important factor determining what happens in the Museum, but there are many different sorts. The largest group consists of those, both British and international, who come or return to look at a famous object such as the Rosetta Stone, to see a special exhibition, or to find out about a particular culture. The 'regular visitor' is not, however, a static group that could ever be taken for granted. There are plenty of other things for people to do or see, so the Museum needs to renew itself constantly as a place that is attractive and interesting while at the same time responding to those with special needs or from particular cultural or social backgrounds. Many children visit, sometimes with their schools and sometimes with their families. Some people come to pursue their own research, and do so in rooms where access to objects not on display is arranged for those who want to see them. Others come with objects that they want identified, or to ask a question. They may also do this by letter, phone or e-mail. The Museum's website is being developed with the same groups of visitors in mind, since the Internet now provides a way of making the Museum available to those who are unable or do not wish to come to London. Parts of the collection also travel physically to other parts of Britain and the world, as long-term loans to other museums and as touring exhibitions.

Changes to the collection, changes to the visitors have both had their impact. So have changes in the staff. The influence of the Museum's Trustees and what would nowadays be called its senior management has, of course, always been paramount; this book sets out to show how the character of the place can also be demonstrated through some of the 900 people who work in the Museum – how they go about their jobs from day to day and what they are trying to achieve. Inevitably it is selective, since we wanted to relate it as far as possible to what the public can see and experience, and to what is distinctive about The British Museum.

10 BEHIND THE SCENES AT THE BRITISH MUSEUM

CHAPTER 1

Looking Back

The word 'museum' comes from the Latin *musaeum*, which means a place dedicated to the Muses, the nine daughters of Memory who were the embodiments of intellectual and artistic achievement in classical myth. The Museum of Alexandria, founded in the third century BC, housed a great library and was a place of scholarship and research. During the Italian Renaissance of the fifteenth century, the popes and princes who wanted to recover the Roman world made many collections of antiquities. The first building constructed as a museum was built in the late sixteenth century. Voyages of discovery meant that collecting the rest of the world soon became as important as collecting the past. But this was not just collecting objects for admiration and aesthetic pleasure. They were gathered for serious study, whether in the humanities or the sciences, and so great museums developed in parallel to great libraries.

How did we get here?

It is curious that, apart from its ancient universities and cathedrals, Britain had no great library or museum before the eighteenth century. 'There is not a great City in Europe so ill provided with Public Libraries as London', wrote Thomas Carte in 1743. Little changed on either front until a doctor called Hans Sloane built up a collection of natural and 'artificial curiosities', a term that covered Roman and Egyptian antiquities, ethnographic specimens, drawings and coins. Sloane's collection was so famous that it was widely visited by the leading politicians, royalty and intellectuals of the day, including Voltaire, Benjamin Franklin, Handel and the future King George III. During his visit George 'express'd the great pleasure it gave him to see so magnificent a collection in England, esteeming it an ornament to the nation; and express'd his sentiments how much it must conduce to the benefit of learning, and how great an honour will redound to Britain, to have it established for publick use to the latest posterity.'

When Sloane died in 1753 his will offered this extraordinary collection to the nation. After a certain amount of vacillating by the government of the day, his offer was accepted. The collection was acquired for the nation and together with two other great collections of manuscripts and books it became the British Museum. 'British' only in the sense that it belonged to the nation. It was at once the national library and national museum that

Sir Hans Sloane (1660–1753), whose collections established The British Museum.

Britain had so long lacked, and became the first public museum in the world.

The contents of the Museum

When the Museum was founded some 250 years ago it was intended to represent the sum of human knowledge. The founding collection of the doctor Sloane included more than 120,000 'plants, fossils, minerals, zoological, anatomical and pathological specimens, antiquities and artificial curiosities, prints, drawings and coins, books and manuscripts'.

Roman sculptures on display in the Wolfson Galleries of Roman Sculpture. The figures in the foreground, from Libya, were acquired in 1861.

Thereafter new emphases can be seen. An interest in Greek and Roman antiquities was the natural result of an educational system based on the classics, and many important collections were acquired: Greek vases from Sir William Hamilton, classical sculpture and bronzes from Charles Townley, and Greek sculpture from Lord Elgin. At the same time important Egyptian objects came, such as the Rosetta Stone (see p. 39), the trilingual inscription that led to the decipherment of Egyptian hieroglyphics and so unlocked Egyptian culture. The discovery of Mesopotamian civilizations and the excitement created because of their relationship with the Bible were reflected by the gift of the Rich collection 'illustrative of countries situated on the Euphrates and the Tigris', and later by the sculpture and cuneiform tablets found in the excavations carried out by Layard and Rawlinson.

By the mid nineteenth century the Museum was dominated by the three themes of the classical world, Egypt and Mesopotamia, as the 1870 *British Museum Guide to the Exhibition Galleries* makes clear: British, medieval and ethnographical displays account for only 7 out of a total of 53 pages. This remains a common perception of the Museum some 150 years later, but there have been many changes since then. Indeed, the position now is akin to that of the founding collections. Although the books and natural history specimens have gone, the Museum today is interested in all the world's cultures and in the relationships between them, not just the ancient ones and not just those originating in the Mediterranean or Middle East.

One of the curiosities of the early nineteenth-century Museum is that little attention was paid to Britain, even though this was the heyday of antiquarianism and the Museum was criticized for this absence. The British collection was small and barely displayed. This was all to change when the young A.W. Franks joined the Museum in 1851. The astonishing energy of this one man during the second half of the nineteenth century brought about a new emphasis not only on Britain, but also many other parts of the world. Franks proudly recorded how he had increased the collections for which he was responsible from a mere '154 feet of wall cases, and 3 or 4 table cases' to '2,250 feet in length of wall cases, 90 table cases and 31 upright cases, to say nothing of the numerous objects placed over the cases or on walls'. As well as British and European material, Franks made many Islamic, Indian, Chinese and Japanese acquisitions, and built up the prehistoric and ethnographical collections from all over the world.

At the same time the removal of the natural history collection to South Kensington meant that the Museum then contained only the products of human civilization, rather than representing knowledge of the world as a whole. The twentieth century witnessed other changes, again giving new emphases to the Museum. The separation of the British Library in 1973 and its move to a new building in St Pancras in 1998 has meant the departure of much written material that illuminates antiquities in the Museum, from documents written in Greek on ancient papyri to illuminated manuscripts from medieval Britain. On the other hand, the removal of the ethnographical collections to the Museum of Mankind has, thankfully, proved to be temporary. The proposed independent Museum of Ethnography was never built and the African, Asian, Australasian and American collections are to be reunited with those of the rest of the world over the next few years.

Over the same period the laws of many countries have progressively restricted the export of antiquities so that very little can nowadays be acquired from overseas. The consequence is that Britain – and, most recently, England – has become the main source of new acquisitions. Other changes, whether on a small scale (such as the decision to collect paper money) or with a larger impact (like the decision to collect contemporary material), occurred for a variety of reasons. In the case of ethnography, it became more important to undertake contextual collecting of objects from societies that were fast disappearing than to add to collections of a known type. Similarly, in the field of art, the purchase of contemporary Japanese or Western prints before they became too expensive ensured that the Museum's collection remained representative. It is now standard practice throughout the Museum to collect contemporary material from all over the world.

In ways like these, changing external circumstances and new internal emphases have led to fundamental changes in the Museum's content. The vicissitudes of history and taste have had their effect. The present conception of a more universal museum, as was embodied in the founding collections, cannot alter the impact of the past 250 years during which specialist institutions were created. The result is that it is rather difficult now to give a clear description of what is in the Museum, except as a series of contrasts. The collections represent the sum of human knowledge, except for the natural and scientific world; they represent the products of human civilization, except for oil paintings and the written word. There are surprises and the unexpected: a superb collection of clocks and watches, and of contemporary political badges. Science may have gone to South Kensington, but there is a collection of early scientific instruments, and numerous members of staff are engaged on the scientific study of the past and the scientific conservation of the collection. There are many inconsistencies: Egyptian papyri are here if they are written in demotic but not if they are written in Greek. There are some overlaps with other national institutions: you can also find Indian art and Western prints in the Victoria and Albert Museum.

Today the collections embrace Europe, the Americas, Africa, Asia and the Pacific, and they include artefacts from cultures as diverse as the Han empire in China and Anglo-Saxon England; from the Palaeolithic period in East Anglia to the work of Rembrandt and his school; from the Umayyad caliphate to twentieth-century Madagascar; and from centralized states to small-scale rural communities. The best advice is to assume something is here until told otherwise (the collections are briefly described department by department on pp. 122–3).

The building, the records and the staff

Apart from the collections, three vital ingredients comprise the Museum as we know it today: the building, the records and the staff.

The present building stands on the site of the Museum's original

Above Montagu House, as rebuilt in
1686: the first home of The British
Museum from 1754.

Below Progress of the new Museum
building, as seen by George Scharf
the Elder in 1828.

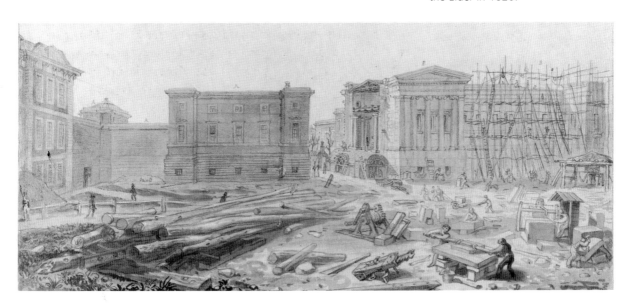

The old and the new: Smirke's classical façade and the international style of Foster's Great Court roof.

home, Montagu House, a seventeenth-century house (see also pp. 61–4). The building was in poor condition when it was bought and rapidly became too small for the expanding collection, despite an extension in 1808. A new building, commissioned from Sir Robert Smirke, one of the leading architects of the day, was constructed over a period of more than 30 years from 1823. It was the largest public building in Britain and was conceived very much as a cathedral to the arts. While many additions have been made over the years, the Smirke building remains the dominant physical expression of the Museum. But if its classical character is a famous landmark, it is also a somewhat overpowering asset. A visual expression of the ideals of the early nineteenth century, it still imposes its identity on anything that happens inside. But today the world of The British Museum, as we have seen, is much wider than classical Greece or ancient Egypt and encompasses all cultures, whether of the past or the present. We also accept that our understanding is more relative. While we would certainly not agree that subjectivity is the only way forward, we have come a long way from believing that there can be an objective approach that is completely divorced from the background of those who might promote it (and which this book will at least in part reveal). The new international architecture embodied in Norman Foster's Great Court of 2000 may perhaps symbolize this change (see p. 105). The façade of the

Museum remains rooted in the nineteenth century, but what goes on inside nowadays extends beyond any one culture or point of view.

Secondly, there are the records, about which it is easy to give the wrong idea. The Museum's records of its own history and the collections it houses are far from a 'dusty accumulation'. Together with books and other information they form part of the resources needed to give context to the Museum's collection. The Museum is not an art gallery, and people do not visit solely for aesthetic enjoyment. We can only use artefacts 'to promote knowledge of the history of civilization' by developing an understanding of the background from which they come. At its simplest, this could be a record of a find-spot or of the archaeological level of an excavation. Or it may be an appreciation of the relationship of a particular artefact to something similar from the same or another culture. This requires books and archives, ranging from papers about the history of the Museum to notes about the watercolourist Tom Girtin or plaster casts of lost Mayan inscriptions. Despite the departure of the British Library, the Museum still has a very large collection of books, such as the specialized numismatic and anthropological libraries it holds (the latter jointly with the Royal Anthropological Institute).

These are some of the tools that the Museum's staff use to help develop our understanding of the collection. The people who work for the Museum have always been a vital component in its operation, since it is their expertise, their ability to look after and interpret the collections and make them available, that is the basis of the way the Museum deals with its public. 'Public' is widely defined: young and old, black and white, British and foreign, scholar and schoolchild, people with learning difficulties, people who use the Internet. The staff have two primary roles in relation to these diverse publics: they must be able to understand what the collections can represent and to communicate this to these different audiences.

This is a serious responsibility, and so the Museum's staff have skills and abilities across a very wide spectrum of subjects. There is a distinguished board of 25 Trustees. There are people who ensure that the finances, buildings and systems of the museum are well managed, its exhibitions well displayed and that the collections are safe. The curators are a distinctive group who cumulatively hold the astonishing knowledge that is the hallmark of the Museum as a whole. They may speak and read obscure languages, they may be the world experts on the objects they look after, they may have been teachers, they may have studied medieval history or conservation science, they often collaborate with colleagues all over the world.

This book seeks to illuminate how those who work there make a particular contribution to the unique institution that is The British Museum. In the following pages, you will find some of the answers to questions about who they are, what they do and why they do it.

CHAPTER 2

Displaying

Ask someone why they are going to a museum and most people will say that it is to see what is on show. The British Museum, like other museums and galleries, puts on a number of special exhibitions every year, but most visitors come to see what is on permanent display. There are famous exhibits that everyone has heard of, such as the Rosetta Stone from Egypt, the Parthenon sculptures from Greece or the Sutton Hoo ship burial from Britain. Many people think of them as individual pieces, but in The British Museum they are displayed in galleries that provide a historical context. Using the objects to help us see into the minds of different societies is a distinctive feature of the way that The British Museum approaches its displays. In this sense, it is primarily a historical rather than an art museum.

Providing a historical context is much more difficult than just putting certain objects out on view, and a lot of thought goes into the preparation of all the Museum's exhibitions. It is always a surprise to anyone working on their first exhibition just how much work, time and money goes into such a project. Obviously, the amount varies depending on the size and complexity of the exhibition, but a new permanent display will often involve a team of 100 people, take two years and have a budget of over £1m. The people who work on these projects include curators, designers, architects, conservators, scientists, illustrators, builders, administrators, engineers, carpenters, educators, editors, photographers, security staff, accountants, stonemasons, IT specialists, volunteers, press officers, fundraisers, locksmiths. Since the Museum has almost 100 galleries, each of which needs rethinking or refurbishing at least once a generation, we can get an idea of the work involved. And, over and above that, the Museum organizes several temporary and travelling exhibitions every year.

In this chapter we look at the development of two permanent galleries, one devoted to the culture of Korea and the other surveying the history of money throughout the world. We also consider two recent special exhibitions: *Cleopatra of Egypt*, which also toured abroad, and *Writing Arabic*, which travelled to several venues around the UK. We could, of course, have chosen any number of other examples. Different aspects have been emphasized in each case, but none the less only a flavour of what is involved can be conveyed in the space available here.

The Korea Foundation Gallery

Korea was closed to foreigners on pain of death until 1880. Consequently, it was not very well known in the West and European understanding of its art and archaeology lagged behind that of the neighbouring civilizations of China and Japan. For the same reason, the Museum's acquisition of Korean objects began only at the very end of the nineteenth century. Like most Western collections of Korean artefacts, the British Museum's is relatively small, although it is the best in Europe, and for several years the Museum had wanted to advance our understanding of this 'Hermit Kingdom'. A temporary loan exhibition in 1984 suggested the idea of a permanent gallery. This was made possible when the Korea Foundation, an arm of the Korean Foreign Ministry, decided in 1992 to fund a gallery. It opened in 2000.

Jane Portal
Oriental Antiquities

'I went off to the School of Oriental and African Studies to study for a BA Hons degree in Korean Studies, at the same time as working full-time in the Museum and having a baby. I then spent an academic year (with two of my three children) living and studying in Seoul. Since I already had a degree in Chinese and had lived in China as a student, I suppose I had a bit of a start, but the Korean language is actually very difficult and the grammar much more complicated than Chinese.

While in Korea I visited as many museums as possible and also started collecting contemporary paintings, prints and ceramics to be displayed on a rotating basis in the new gallery. I was supported and encouraged by many Korean scholars and artists, who were delighted that their country would be permanently represented in The British Museum. Visiting temples and other traditional buildings inspired me to try and recreate such a building in the Museum – just as we have a traditional tea room in the Japanese gallery. The Korea Foundation agreed to fund the re-creation of a *sarangbang* or gentleman's study, complete with furniture. A similar one is on display in the National Museum of Korea, whose director kindly recommended craftsmen to make the particular furniture needed.

While studying in Korea I also met Mr Hahn Kwang-ho, who has since become the British Museum's first Korean Patron. His donation of a large purchase fund for Korean art has helped me to build up the collection in new areas. We were all delighted when he was honoured with the CBE by the Queen on her state visit to Korea in 1999.

One of my other main tasks in the preparation of the Korean gallery has been the publication of an 80,000-word book on Korean art and archaeology, which I hope will introduce the general public to the history and beauty of Korean art.'

Responsibility for the intellectual vision behind a display rests with the relevant specialist or team of curators, and colleagues from other institutions may be involved. The British Library has played an important part in the development of the Korean gallery, both by lending some of the Library's rich collection of Korean books and albums for the display and by contributing expertise to the project.

Beth McKillop
British Library

'I studied Chinese at Cambridge in the 1970s, and took courses in Korean at London University in the 1980s. My work today involves researching and cataloguing a collection of rare books and manuscripts, as well as selecting contemporary Korean material for the Library. I'm also exhibitions and loans officer for the Asian materials in the British Library, and so I know the British Museum's Department of Oriental Antiquities well.

Working with Jane Portal on the Korean gallery has been a big part of my job for over 10 years now. I've lost count of the number of journeys I made between my former office in south London and The British Museum, bringing books, scrolls and albums for display. When the Library moved to St Pancras in 1998, things became much easier for me, and I began to think about the gallery opening in 2000. We have needed to consider many things, practicalities like how long a delicate manuscript should be exposed to the light and whether visitors to the gallery would get the point of an archaic Korean map portraying the world as a kind of doughnut-shaped ring surrounded by sea.

In the new gallery we've made a selection that includes part of the Buddhist Canon, which is a kind of national icon in Korea and is preserved in a beautiful, remote mountain temple that I am determined to visit one day. We're also trying to convey something of the regional diversity of Korea, much in the news today because it seems that finally the division of the country into communist north and capitalist south may be coming to an end. I'm sure that the permanent gallery will fulfil its purpose of introducing the quiet, quirky beauty of Korean art to the Museum's visitors and I'm looking forward to the next stage – more display plans, more trips with suitcases between the British Library and The British Museum.'

As well as colleagues with specific skills and expertise, such projects sometimes offer outsiders a unique opportunity to become part of a museum. In this case, a committed student with a deep knowledge of Korean culture provided the Museum with invaluable assistance.

Moonjung Choi
Oriental Antiquities

'I first came to The British Museum in the summer of 1998 to work as a volunteer in the temporary Korean gallery when I had just started my graduate studies in Korean Art History in Ewha University in Seoul. The opportunity to work in The British Museum was exciting as it gave me a chance to look at what real museum work was like. I returned in the following winter and worked on the COMPASS project [see p. 109], writing the introductions to Korean objects.

It was, however, great to return in 2000 to work on the permanent Korean gallery. Part of my work was to interpret for and look after the needs and

Building the *sarangbang* in the Korea Foundation Gallery.

well-being of the ten Korean workmen who built the *sarangbang* or scholar's studio. All the materials, such as the pine wood, roof tiles and granite, were shipped from Korea. These leading Korean traditional craftsmen had planned to build the *sarangbang* in less than three weeks, working to a very tight schedule. Their efficiency was amazing. Although they had drawn a plan and specific measurements had been made, they rarely needed to glance at the drawings. They had reached a point in their craftsmanship that their eyes and hands knew the exact measurements and the details of the plan. When I asked them whether a certain pillar was giving them a little difficulty, the craftsmen replied that everything they built was different, so they were not troubled or perplexed by what to do, they would work with it.

Although my assistance to the *sarangbang* workmen was only part of my work in the Museum, it was perhaps the most inspirational. My short involvement in the building of the *sarangbang* in The British Museum has given me a more three-dimensional view of the efforts of the many people who work together to create a display.'

Although some members of the team may be working exclusively on the project, others might be juggling many diverse activities. One of the

Museum's photographers explains how he became involved in the Korean gallery (see also p. 106):

Dudley Hubbard
Photography and Imaging

'What started as a hobby has now become my profession and I still get a kick from making new images and seeing the results. My colleague Simon Tutty and I provide a general photography service to the whole Museum covering any subjects that do not come under the remit of our academic department photographers. In effect we are press photographers.

Both the Design Office and the Oriental Antiquities Department wanted daily progress shots to illustrate some of the techniques being used in the construction of the *sarangbang*. I selected a view that I felt would provide a good general overview and as best I could used the same lens and view each day I attended. On top of this, I wanted to get in with the action and so I shot some 'open flash' images (hand-held, slow shutter-speed, with flash) of the carpenters sawing and hammering. This gave a good impression of life and movement in the images and is favoured by many who use and view photography today. With any project like this, the whole story is constructed by chipping away at every opportunity so that at the end of the three weeks there is a collection of material to choose from. These images will go on to advertise our museum and attract more visitors; they will also educate and inspire further audiences and already they make up a little part of the history of this wonderful place.

Photography remains a very important integral part of any museum, ours being no exception. Not only the recording of objects, which I haven't even touched on here, but also in constructing a historical insight based around the daily life and times of a public space/building. As well as the enjoyable part of photography there are the meticulous records that have to be maintained in order to ensure that the images illustrate a historical coherency of dates and places.'

HSBC Money Gallery

Whereas most of the Museum's exhibitions look at a particular culture or period, some are devoted to a specific theme. This enables the similarities and differences between cultures to be explored. A recent example of this approach is the gallery about the history of money, which opened in 1997. Although the final result is very different from the Korean gallery, the organization of the project was similar in many ways. The gallery had a team of curators, and also called on those with architectural and design skills. Like the Korean gallery, the conception of the project included a book, and, more unusually, a CD-Rom (although these days almost any museum exhibition project has a digital component or web presence).

The Museum was left without a means of presenting its world-class numismatic collection to the public when a fire-bomb destroyed its display area during the Second World War (see p. 86). In the late 1980s a space that could become a permanent gallery for the Coins and Medals Department was identified. However, it took another decade before that possibility became a reality, when HSBC Holdings agreed to provide the Museum with a donation that would cover the costs of refitting the space for the display of the collections. The principal curator of the HSBC Money Gallery describes its ambitious scope, and how it managed to present a complicated story in a way that visitors could understand:

Joe Cribb
Coins and Medals

'When I joined it in 1970, one of the first things I was told was that the department was hoping to open its own permanent display as soon as possible. After almost 30 years of living with this dream, I was delighted to be asked to head the curatorial team that created the new display. In accepting this role I was determined to place our collection on show in a way that the

General view of the HSBC Money Gallery.

Museum's visitors would understand and enjoy. I decided that the aspect of our collection that would be most familiar to all visitors was the role of coins and banknotes as money in everyday life. The theme of the new gallery was the history of money, from its earliest manifestations right down to the present day. By including the money of today, I wanted to provide a familiar starting point for visitors to engage with the display.

It was my hope that the public would be able to understand why coins and banknotes were invented by showing them alongside the more recent invention of computerized money and bank cards, to understand why Alexander the Great was represented on Greek coins by showing them alongside British coins representing Elizabeth II, and to understand why the ancient Chinese buried clay copies of gold ingots with their dead by showing them alongside the silver threepence pieces my mother buried in the Xmas puddings she served up to me as a child.'

The realization of any such aspiration depends on having the resources to put it into practice. Many years ago the Museum was mostly funded by the Government, but this has long since changed and nowadays any gallery project needs an outside sponsor or donor. In this case, HSBC Holdings donated some £2 million, a gift that was solicited by the Museum's fundraising arm, The British Museum Development Trust.

Julian Marland
Development Trust

'I joined the Trust in 1994, having left a career in corporate banking with a large American bank in the City. Although this may seem an odd background for a museum fundraiser, the similarities in what I actually do day-to-day are quite strong. Fundraising is essentially a sales and marketing job, even though what we are 'selling' is a lot more interesting and worthwhile than banking services.

Much of the work of the Trust spins off from a weekly team meeting, usually chaired by our Chairman, Sir Claus Moser, and attended by the Museum's Chairman, Graham Greene. At this we review the list of prospects and try to match them up against the list of projects which require funding. We then try to work out how we are going to approach the various prospects, or review progress where the approach has already started, and agree next steps. We also review the various events we organize to check that we are getting the most out of them. When we were considering the Money Gallery, the contacts the Museum had and the recent formation of HSBC Holdings as a British company suggested that it might be a natural partner.

Day-to-day work is similar to many 'office' jobs with lots of meetings, both internal and external. I spend a lot of time talking to colleagues within the Museum to ensure that the proposals we send out make sense and can be delivered. There are also the crunch meetings, and I well remember the day when we went to the head offices of HSBC to put our proposals to the Chairman and other members of its board!

Apart from that, one of the best features of the job is the interaction with so many different areas of the Museum. Since joining the Museum I have gained an understanding of the management of complex building projects such as the Great Court and IT projects such as COMPASS [see p. 109], as well as the huge range of curatorial activity. I don't think I have a favourite area of the collections; it is the universality of The British Museum that appeals to me, and I think to many of our donors.'

Once the concept and the financing are secure, work can progress on all aspects of the project, including the design and building of the exhibition. The designer, who is concerned with the presentation of the exhibition, needs to work closely with the architect, who is responsible for providing the infrastructure. They both need to be sensitive to the architecture of a Grade 1 listed building while creating an installation that will work well. The designer of the HSBC Money Gallery became involved with the project almost two years before the planned opening.

Jon Ould
Exhibitions and Design

'Although I have been a designer of museum exhibitions and galleries for many years, the HSBC Money Gallery was a real challenge. Unlike other projects, where one region of the world or one time-span is involved, this had to present the broad historical and geographical story of money in what was a fairly restricted space of 200 square metres.

The first stage was to develop a suitable layout of showcases and display areas, which would accommodate the objects in a safe, secure environment and present a logical storyline. The existing architecture must be respected and, working within the Museum's house style (formulated over many years), the process was guided with frequent meetings, discussions and presentations. Timetables, budgets, colour schemes, finishes, lighting and much else had to be agreed before the architect could refurbish and modernize the gallery as required.

The detailed content could then be worked on and I could begin drawing the showcases to be ordered. There were far more objects available than could possibly fit in the gallery and there was much discussion between myself and the curators, helped along by the editor and graphic designer. We made many mock-ups to determine the best position to display coins, finally deciding on a steep slope at a suitable eye-level for the majority of visitors. It was found that backcloth colours which gave less contrast with the coins were the most suitable for seeing the detail, with direct overhead lighting to bring out the relief. Information panels were designed to run above and below the display areas to keep the maximum space available for the objects.

My job is to see the project through to completion. Once the building work is finished and the showcases are installed, the opening date looms, but that is when the most enjoyable part starts: seeing the objects and displays going in. Months of work by many people then come to fruition; it is a very satisfying experience.'

The architect talks of the problems and rewards of working with older and historic buildings:

Satvinder Jandu
Operations

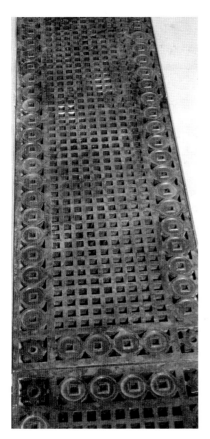

Ventilation grille in HSBC Money Gallery: the ironwork pattern includes the shape of a Chinese coin, making a small architectural joke.

'Having graduated as an architect, I started out in private practice working on a variety of new developments. Whilst this work was interesting, I soon discovered that working with older and historic buildings in particular was extremely challenging and rewarding. I had seen the light!

The opportunity to work in the architectural department at The British Museum was just too good to miss. The major difference between private practice and here was that I wasn't practising hands-on architecture, but co-ordinating a lot of others in delivering projects. It is incredibly exciting to deal with existing structures and the attendant constraints demand a very different kind of creative energy. You cannot always start from scratch, so you need architectural strategies that are not primarily motivated by taste and stylistic preferences. The strategy that evolved in the development of the Money Gallery was based on the desire to respect and enhance the character and quality of the space, in a manner befitting a Grade 1 listed building. The architectural issues were fairly clear but, as modern galleries demand a highly controlled environment for reasons of conservation and visitor comfort, the major challenge was to integrate the plethora of services, both inside and outside the space, in a discreet and sympathetic fashion. It is also vital to look ahead and ensure that new services dovetail into the Museum's wider scheme of things.

With the development strategies in place, the next task was to appoint a team of consultants to develop the proposals to obtain consents and to implement the scheme to the usual tight deadline (with a fixed opening date) and strict cost levels. Selecting the right architect, support consultants and construction team is vital to the success of any project. We were fortunate to engage consultants who collaborated and meshed well with the Museum's project team, which included curators, 3D designers, editors and conservation scientists. This is not to say that relations didn't get tense at times, particularly in the approach to completion!

Given the complex construction logistics of working in an occupied and working museum, it is fair to say we come under extreme pressure once work commences. Apart from fielding regular complaints about noise and dust, a big concern is ensuring the safety of nearby objects, staff and visitors. In the final analysis, it is extremely gratifying to see thousands, indeed millions, of visitors from all corners of the world enjoying a space that one has played a small part in creating.'

Once the gallery had opened, HSBC also provided financial support for two related aspects of the project. The first was the production of an interactive CD-Rom. The curator who wrote and co-ordinated the project recalls the process of developing it.

Gareth Williams
Coins and Medals

'As a specialist in Anglo-Saxon and Viking history, it came as something of a shock when my first major project for The British Museum was to put together a CD-Rom as part of the HSBC Money Gallery project. Multimedia is now increasingly used by museums to make their collections more accessible to the public, but *World of Money* was the BM's first big multimedia project and nobody knew quite what to expect.

Multimedia offers many advantages when dealing with small objects like coins. It is possible to show enlarged images, which makes the objects easier to identify and read. At the same time, particularly interesting details can be highlighted, such as the security marks on a banknote or the moneyer's name on a medieval coin. Video and animations allowed us to show how different types of money have been produced from ancient times to the present day, and also the different ways in which money is used, from shopping during the January sales to the Hong Kong Stock Exchange. We were also able to include games and activities that bring the subject alive, including designing money and running the economy of a city-state.

Children exploring a money chest on a 'money trail' in the HSBC Money Gallery.

World of Money covers the history of money over the past five thousand years across the whole world, and one of the most exciting things for me was trying to plan a structure that gave the right amount of information about all sorts of areas I knew nothing about. Fortunately, I did not have to write everything myself and between us the 17 contributors were able to cover all the appropriate material (I think!). However, this brought the additional challenge of editing all the different contributions into a consistent style. Some authors wrote very clearly and simply, but others were egregiously sesquipedalian. In the end, we produced something that I think we can be proud of, with around 200,000 words of text and over 2,000 images. More importantly, we learned a great deal from the experience of making it, so that future multimedia projects in the BM can be even better.'

HSBC also generously provided support for a development curator, whose role is to make sure that the public get as much from their visit to the gallery as possible. This means ensuring that the display is working and makes sense to visitors, and also providing additional resources that help bring the objects to life (see also Chapter 5).

John Orna-Ornstein
Coins and Medals

'I've often thought that it is only when the last object is placed in a gallery and the exhibition opens to the public that the real work begins. Galleries are as much about the people who use them as they are about objects in exhibition cases.

Any gallery can be improved. One of the first things we did with the HSBC Money Gallery was to evaluate it. We watched how visitors used the gallery, and asked them what they liked and disliked about the displays. We also commissioned experts to assess how easy it was for people to understand and use the exhibition. This process of evaluation highlighted a number of areas that could be improved, and over the following two years we made several small changes to the gallery. Of course, it is still not perfect, and we plan to update and modify the displays regularly throughout the gallery's lifetime.

Many visitors like to do more than look at objects in cases when they visit the Museum. Unlike Greek sculpture or Egyptian mummies, coins and banknotes were literally made to be handled, and we frequently give visitors the opportunity to hold and explore ancient and modern material from the department's teaching collections. We also deliver a range of talks in the gallery and provide trails and leaflets that help adults and children alike to get more out of the displays. These services are particularly important for people – ranging from children to visually impaired visitors – who find traditional displays difficult to use. Our intention is to make sure that the HSBC Money Gallery is an interesting, exciting and vibrant place for all our visitors!'

Cleopatra of Egypt

Every year the Museum presents a number of special exhibitions lasting three or four months. The purpose of a special exhibition is to show ideas or themes that cannot easily be treated in the permanent galleries. In the past few years the programme has included exhibitions about such diverse subjects as the Rosetta Stone (see p. 39), mummy portraits from Roman Egypt, new archaeological discoveries from China, and Cartier jewellery 1900–39.

The opening of the Great Court in late 2000 has enabled the Museum to put on twice as many special exhibitions. One of the first was devoted to that famous beauty (according to some), Cleopatra. Taking recent archaeological discoveries in Egypt as a starting-point, the exhibition reassessed the famous queen and lover of Julius Caesar and Mark Antony. *Cleopatra of Egypt* also travelled to Rome and Chicago and is a good example of how the Museum's work has an impact on an international audience. Not only do millions of visitors come from abroad, but the Museum also sends its collections and expertise around the world.

Susan Walker
Greek and Roman Antiquities

A portrait of Cleopatra in the Greek manner, on a very rare silver coin of Ascalon (modern Ashkelon, Israel).

'As a postgraduate student working on Roman architecture in Greece, I had it in mind to abandon my suitcase for a university which would offer me a tranquil library where I could write up my research. It was with some surprise that, armed only with detailed knowledge of the sites from which the mountain of marble sculpture came, I instead began a career as a curator of Roman antiquities at The British Museum.

My first exhibition was *The Image of Augustus*, an exploration of the sources of the public image of the first Roman emperor, an appealing theme in the years following the then unprecedented marketing of Mrs Thatcher as Prime Minister. Since then I have prepared several permanent galleries of Greek sculpture and Roman antiquities. However, I never lost my interest in portraiture, and was delighted to be invited to prepare the catalogue of the 1997 special exhibition on mummy portraits, *Ancient Faces*. This exhibition travelled to Rome, where its success was such that the President of the Fondazione Memmo, which had supported the exhibition, pressed for a follow-up. Cleopatra seemed a suitable if challenging subject, and one suited to the millennium year, since her suicide changed the course of the history of the Western world.

I was keen to develop a biographical exhibition, rather like the earlier work on Augustus, a show that would start and end with questions. I wanted the visitor to ask 'who was Cleopatra?' and to leave the exhibition asking 'who's *my* Cleopatra?', taking in the multitude of images of the Egyptian queen developed during and since her remarkable lifetime.

Researching the exhibition was a revelation: no one could have imagined how much more there was still to know about so famous a figure. Making it happen was a more challenging proposition, one that can only be achieved with the collaboration of a huge group of people. This is the most exciting end of the spectrum of curatorial work: I am very privileged to experience it, and I have constantly learned new skills in the process of bringing this exhibition about.'

Some of the excitement of the new discoveries can be felt:

Sally-Ann Ashton
Greek and Roman Antiquities

'I came to The British Museum to work as a Special Assistant five years ago. On the days that I wasn't registering pottery, I was researching and writing my doctoral thesis on the royal sculpture of Ptolemaic Egypt. In the six months following my completion of the pottery register, and while I began to write up my research on the sculpture, the exhibition on Cleopatra had been conceived. My involvement with the exhibition from the very start offered me a unique opportunity to present my research to the public and to gather and reunite material from many museums across the world.

The exhibition also forced me to think carefully about re-dating and re-attributing representations, in both Greek and Egyptian styles, of Cleopatra and her forefathers. Putting ideas down on paper might provoke disagreement but is relatively cheap; the costs of assembling material for special exhibitions requires the academic groundwork to be based on a solid footing. Ideas that started as conjecture were, with the help of colleagues and the opportunity to visit and work in museums in America, Europe and Egypt, developed into theories supported by strong evidence.

During my work for the exhibition, I discovered seven new representations of Cleopatra. The greatest surprise was a small glass gem in our own department at The British Museum, which proved to be the missing link supporting my proposed identification of the Egyptian-style images of Cleopatra.

My most lasting memory of the exhibition is the collaboration with the many different colleagues who have been involved. The result was certainly a team effort that would put the rivalry and murderous antics of Cleopatra's family to shame.'

Because special exhibitions last for only a few months, it is possible to borrow material to complement the Museum's own holdings. Other institutions do not usually want to deprive their own collections of important objects for long, so are prepared to lend only for a short time. As *Cleopatra of Egypt* was also being shown in Rome and Chicago, the job of organizing the loans from many different sources was enormous. Legal, technical, transport, conservation and security matters all have to be taken into account, as does cost. The movement of irreplaceable archaeological treasures around the world requires great care and considerable expense.

Evelyn Wood
Greek and Roman Antiquities

'I was involved in the Cleopatra project from 1998 as team leader for the administrative staff. From the early stages my role involved keeping accounts, ordering goods and services, and making travel arrangements for project members travelling to Egypt, the United States, Italy and to museums, universities and libraries within the UK. This was an extension of my normal duties within the department, as was the process of exchanging formal agreements with other institutions for objects to be loaned to and from the Museum.

With nine years' experience of administering loans out for the Museum, I was able to contribute advice to project members on established practice and regulations. In addition, they could draw on my contacts with administrators in other museums and galleries, transport companies and government departments who might be needed to assist with movement of objects and couriers.

Cleopatra of Egypt was by far the largest exhibition project I have worked on, and a rare opportunity to be involved in the organization of incoming loans from collections all over the world. Corresponding with prospective lenders has offered a fascinating insight into just how difficult it can be to provide certain details while the exhibition is still in the design phase. This has certainly given me more of an understanding into some of the delays I have experienced when we have requested information from exhibition organizers wishing to borrow from us!'

Once the selection of objects has been made, one of the most important tasks is conservation. The objects may need cleaning and all need to be assessed to see if they are sufficiently stable for display and travel. Fashions change and old conservation treatments or restorations need to be re-examined.

Karen Birkhoelzer
Conservation

'The work carried out by the Stone, Wall-Painting and Mosaics Section for the Cleopatra exhibition often presented unique challenges. The nature of the subject required the treatment of objects from two curatorial departments, and many of the objects were stored in basements and were not currently on display. Every object had to be assessed individually first for stability and suitability to be displayed, and then for potential travel to Rome and on to Chicago after having been displayed at The British Museum. Such travelling exhibitions put the objects under a lot of stress through continuous handling and conservators have to consider their treatment carefully with that in mind.

There were also aesthetic issues to be considered. After liaising with the curators from both departments, it was decided that new mounts were often required and many old restorations had to be removed and sometimes replaced. Many of the objects also needed to be cleaned. While removing many layers of old dirt the conservator may sometimes discover traces of ancient paint layers. These can be analysed by the Museum's scientists and can help the curators to understand the wider issues of academic interest.

Designers at each venue, as well as the Museum's own curators, have specific ideas about how to display an object and conservators have to liaise with them and supervise the use of materials. Certain materials can react with one another and cause adhesives to fail, thus posing a threat of damage.

Conservation is an integral part of an exhibition not only because it ensures the safety of the objects, but also because it helps the detailed study and understanding of important pieces and the presentation of new material to the public. The result is satisfying for all.'

Writing Arabic

The British Museum organizes travelling exhibitions in collaboration with other UK museums as a way of enabling the collections to reach a wider geographical audience and in order to support the work of colleagues in regional museums and complement their collections. *Writing Arabic* has worked well because it is a theme that would not be easy for another museum to organize on its own, and because of the close collaboration between the Museum's staff and those from other museums.

The exhibition was first displayed in a small gallery in The British Museum in 1997–8, and study days, calligraphy sessions with the Iraqi calligrapher Mustafa Ja'far, were organized by the Education Department for adults and children. With the enthusiastic support of colleagues, especially Carolyn Perry in the Education Department, and with funds from the Heritage Lottery Fund and the Karim Rida Said Foundation, the exhibition and a package of educational activities went to the Royal Albert Memorial Museum in Exeter, the Museum of East Asian Art in Bath, The Ulster Museum in Belfast and finally to the Oriental Museum in Durham. A spin-off was that some of the work done by children in Exeter and elsewhere was later displayed at The British Museum in the exhibition *Arab Cultures: Young Worlds* (see pp. 114–15).

Venetia Porter
Oriental Antiquities

The 'Hand of Fatima' (daughter of the prophet Muhammad), used to protect against evil.

'*Writing Arabic* grew out of my increasing fascination with the Arabic script as a result of my work on Islamic coins and seals. The aim was to use Arabic script, which appears on a myriad of 'Islamic' objects, as a window into the culture of Islam. Using coins, ceramics, monumental inscriptions, amulets and car stickers,[1] different topics were addressed: the origins of the Arabic script, the different styles of writing that developed, and the way in which the Arabic script was imitated in Renaissance Europe. The spread of Islam to its furthest point in South-east Asia was looked at from the point of view of the many languages across the world, geographically as far apart as Persian and Javanese, which all use the Arabic script. In a section called 'The Power of the Word', I included amulets inscribed with Qur'anic inscriptions as well as mysterious letters and magical squares. A section on Muslims in China was an opportunity to display some fine examples of blue-and-white porcelain and bronzes with Arabic inscriptions from the Museum's collection. The most eye-catching section of the exhibition was entitled 'The Art of the Calligrapher' for which we borrowed four beautiful manuscripts from the well-known contemporary Sudanese calligrapher, Osman Waqiallah. Trained by a master calligrapher in Egypt, he has a remarkable ability to work in a style that is both traditional and strikingly modern. He also lent us his grandfather's writing board, an object used by children when learning to write and memorize the Qur'an. One of the striking aspects about this exhibition was learning how little people knew about Islamic culture before they came and how much 'Islamophobia' exists. The most gratifying feature was how interested people became in the subject once they started looking. What was fun about doing this was that it was a true partnership, not only between myself as curator and Carolyn with her extraordinary energy and enthusiasm, but also between the curators of the collaborating museums, designers, editors, photographers and museum assistants, without whom, however good the idea, nothing at all can happen.'

Thanks to the interest and collaboration of colleagues in Exeter, the exhibition was displayed as part of the new World Cultures galleries at the Royal Albert Memorial Museum from June to September 1999. The opening of the new galleries was the culmination of a £1.7m project supported by the Heritage Lottery Fund, providing a completely refurbished space for the museum's ethnographic collections. *Writing Arabic* was the first special exhibition in the space within the galleries designated for changing displays.

Len Pole
Royal Albert Memorial Museum,
Exeter

'The principal objective of the new galleries is to increase understanding between the communities from which visitors come and those represented by the collections. The collaboration with The British Museum exhibition made a substantial contribution to the World Cultures galleries project in three ways. First, it served to augment the presentation of information about aspects of Islam, an important element in the new galleries and one that is at present not strongly represented by our own collection. Secondly, it gave the museum an opportunity to link with one of the few organized ethnic groups in Exeter. Thirdly, it provided a springboard for a significant activities' programme, which included a study day on Arabic calligraphy, handling sessions and talks.

The exhibition encouraged the development of a very fruitful relationship with the Islamic Centre for the South West, which is located in the city, particularly through activities co-ordinated by Lucy Mackeith, a freelance museum education specialist with previous experience of working with the collections. She encouraged participation by young members of the Centre in workshops associated with the exhibition and this resulted in some of their work being displayed in The British Museum later in the year. *Writing Arabic* thus demonstrated the possibilities for forging links between regional and national museums, to the benefit of both.'

Moving objects from one location and installing them in an exhibition in another place is not a simple procedure. It requires care and patience, and the Museum depends on the expertise and experience of its staff to ensure that objects travel safely and are remounted properly for exhibition. The courier and mounter for *Writing Arabic* explains how the exhibits travelled to Northern Ireland:

David Owen
Coins and Medals

'The ferry arrived three and a half hours late, due to bad weather in the Irish Sea. It was 16 December 1999, and the exhibition was set to open in Belfast on the 20th. We had packed everything in Bath the previous day. Objects that were small and fragile had been individually and carefully placed in little boxes surrounded by foam padding, and then locked safely into a wooden crate. We covered text panels and boards with bubblewrap and brown tape, then everything was packed securely in the lorry ready for the long journey to Liverpool docks.

The overnight crossing was rough, but my colleague and I were pleased

Coins

Part of the *Writing Arabic* travelling exhibition on display in The Ulster Museum.

that we managed to get some sleep. We had to be wide awake in the morning to help unload the lorry at our destination, The Ulster Museum.

The gallery and cases were ready for installation, and my job was to unpack the Coins and Medals objects and to sort out where each item belonged. I had brought with me a light hammer, small and large black pins, double-sided tape and a tape measure. Most of the display boards from the Bath exhibition were used with few design changes. This meant that many of the pins were already in place, although some pieces had to be remounted to fit the design of the new display cases.

Some objects, particularly the seals, are very small. These had to be delicately mounted with the pins placed in such a way as to be secure, but not to dominate or obscure the object. Banknotes and 'The Hand of Fatima' stickers were attached to the boards with acetate strips at either end, or across the top and bottom. Where there was a danger of damaging coins, I placed polythene tubing over the pins. Finally, I carefully fixed the information labels using double-sided tape.

I enjoyed my trip to Belfast, although it was hard work, and I even managed to do some Christmas shopping before the flight back to London!'

CHAPTER 3

Understanding

Explaining how objects help us to understand the past or present is never a passive activity, since the very process of examining or inter-preting the Museum's collections constantly leads to new discoveries and the reassessment of current knowledge. This is why, over the years, leading scholars have been attracted to the Museum; it is their natural thirst for new knowledge and desire to make it available to others that underpins so many of the Museum's other activities. Every exhibition marks a new advance, every object brought in for identification by one of the Museum's specialists may lead to a new discovery or at least some new information.

Directions of research may differ greatly, according to the field. For some areas, ancient Central Asia for example, we are still discovering basic information about the people who lived there. When did they live? Who were their rulers? How extensive were their territories? Posing these and similar questions continually produces new information. And this is true not just for distant places – the same sorts of questions are asked about Britain for the time before the invasion of the Romans in the first century AD. In other fields a much longer history of research might lead to a different kind of enquiry, producing a study into the extent of the Roman economy, say, or the reception of classical antiquity in the Renaissance. Investigation of how an object was originally made may lead to a greater understanding of technology, and changes in the composition of its materials over several millennia may need detailed conservation research.

In a direct or indirect way, the collections provide the starting-point for nearly all the research carried out in the Museum, and this research covers a wide spectrum. It might include the stylistic appraisal of the motifs of a certain sort of pottery, or the association of an artefact with a particular written text, or determining the exact composition of a series of coins by scientific analysis. It might involve comparing and contrasting the holdings of The British Museum with related collections in other museums. It might be undertaken in response to new archaeological discoveries, whether made by chance or through planned excavation and fieldwork. The second vital ingredient in research is the questions that curators and others ask about the societies represented by the collection; we don't study the objects 'just because they are there', but because we are trying to understand something new. And as interests change, so do the questions asked.

In this chapter we try to give a flavour of just some of the research topics that have been pursued recently in the Museum and the different approaches they use. However, research is not carried out in a vacuum, and it is only worth doing if the results can be presented to many audiences through the use of appropriate media, whether display, written or digital. These methods enable us to reach various audiences, whether the general public (British and international), the academic world, children, people with learning difficulties. These groups may visit an exhibition, read a book or academic article in a peer-reviewed journal, or surf the web. Conferences, study days, and other events add to this package (see Chapter 5). Usually a research project will employ more than one method to share its findings, in order to offer something to several of these groups.

Exhibitions, covered in the previous chapter, are perhaps the most visible means by which the Museum can show how looking at objects can help us understand cultures in other times or in other parts of the world. But they are only one way, and books or articles (whether printed or electronic) are also very important. Books have advantages and disadvantages over exhibitions. Generally speaking, more people see an exhibition (over 5 million a year visit The British Museum, and a special exhibition may attract as many as 150,000 visitors) than will read a book about the topic of the exhibition. The immediacy of the objects on display brings ancient Egypt or medieval England to life in a way that a book never can. Seeing the objects, we instinctively or emotionally feel nearer to the culture that produced them. But a book offers the opportunity to cover a topic in much greater detail, since it is never possible to include more than a few words on a display label. Books can also be aimed at a variety of audiences, such as children, students, or those unable to visit the Museum itself. The production of books and other publications, such as those in electronic media and articles in academic journals, is a distinctive feature of the Museum.

Here we take some examples of research and its publication, looking at a selection of work on ancient scripts, human remains, craft and technology, art and sculpture in the modern period and finally archaeology and fieldwork. It need hardly be added that work in the Museum covers many, many other periods and cultures and it would have been easy to double or treble the length of this chapter.

Ancient scripts

Some of the earliest known documents were written in cuneiform script on clay tablets in ancient Mesopotamia. Since their initial decipherment in the middle of the nineteenth century, they have provided an extraordinary wealth of information about the history of long-lost kingdoms and biblical figures. But the preservation of these archives is not a simple procedure, and the Museum has been conducting research into ways of improving the firing treatments used to conserve the tablets.

David Thickett
Conservation

'The British Museum is an exciting place to work as a conservation scientist. Its collections contain almost every conceivable material, and studying their deterioration and improving their conservation presents many interesting challenges. The complex nature of the work often requires collaboration between experts in different fields. Cuneiform tablets are made from an unfired clay, with the ancient Mesopotamian script inscribed into their surfaces. The tablets tell us about many aspects of life in ancient Mesopotamia 5,000 years ago, from curses and crop yields to diplomatic correspondence and astronomy. For a number of years the tablets have been conserved by firing, like pottery, but to a lower temperature. This strengthens them and allows them to be safely handled by researchers.

To improve this process, I first analysed the clay the tablets were made from. It was quite an unusual material and I worked with Dr Marianne Odlhya's thermal methods laboratory at Birkbeck College in the University of London to measure and understand how the clay behaves when heated. This collaboration suggested modifications that would reduce the number of tablets damaged during firing. The most important was that we could get almost 90 per cent of the strength for the fired tablets by firing to a temperature 100°C lower than was previously used, thus avoiding a potentially damaging reaction when calcite in the tablets decomposes. After thorough testing, the moment of truth arrived with the first firing of actual tablets at the new temperature. Thankfully, they survived the new regime, but much more importantly the batch of tablets underwent 75 per cent less damage than a comparative batch fired according to the old method. Consultation with curators verified that the essential properties of the tablets were retained after conservation. Improving the conservation of this important archive and window into the past has been a very satisfying experience.'

The study of lost languages continues today. It is a generation or so since Linear B and Mayan script were deciphered, although one of the most exciting decipherments ever happened in the nineteenth century. Unlocking ancient Egyptian civilization was made possible by the unique evidence of a text from the second century BC that contained parallel texts in Greek, hieroglyphic and demotic – the 'pierre de granite noire chargée de trois bandes de charactères hyeroglyphiques Grecs et Egyptiens trouvée à Rosette' or, as we know it, the Rosetta Stone. The bicentenary of its discovery was marked by a special exhibition, *Cracking Codes*.

Richard Parkinson
Egyptian Antiquities

'I became an Egyptologist because of a childhood interest in Egyptian texts and one poem in particular. I saw inside the Department of Egyptian Antiquities for the first time when I was 10, so it is rather strange to be

The Rosetta Stone being examined by Eric Miller, who undertook its recent conservation.

working here now. I trained at Oxford and then taught there; I've specialized in the role of poetry in Egyptian culture, drawing on New Historicist literary criticism. The working day is always too short, so that academic things like research, university teaching and external examining tend to happen at weekends.

In 1999 the Museum celebrated the bicentenary of the discovery of the Rosetta Stone with a temporary exhibition, and it was wonderful to work on the object that was the key to deciphering hieroglyphs. The Stone was the obvious centre of the exhibition, and I decided that we should radically redisplay it as the monument that it is; however, I also wanted to show that interpreting texts is not just a matter of mechanically decoding a set of signs and also that every text is an artefact of its culture. I tried to remind people that hieroglyphs are much more than strange pictures, and that they record the sounds of the ancient language. The collection is full of ancient voices and ideas as well as artefacts.

When I chose the 205 objects to illustrate these ideas, I tried to use pieces that hadn't been seen recently (since only part of the Museum's collection of 110,000 Egyptian objects can ever be on display at any one time) in order to highlight some of our less famous treasures as well as the Stone. The exhibits ranged from some of the earliest known examples of writing to a model of the European Space Agency's projected space probe, which is named after the Stone. Egyptology is developing very rapidly, much faster than many popular books suggest, and I wanted to show the visitor the results and implications of this research. Recent theory has foregrounded the subjective lived experience of the past; I wanted to show that the ancient Egyptians were human, not dry and dusty as academics have sometimes made them, and so we included as many ancient jokes and cartoons as we could. My own favourite piece in the exhibition was an ancient schoolboy's copy of the masterpiece of Egyptian poetry, *The Tale of Sinuhe* (the poem that inspired me to become an Egyptologist). To convey visually the idea that everyone 'rewrites' a text as they read it, and that all interpretation of the past is inevitably an appropriation by the modern viewer, we juxtaposed the poem and a poster of the 1950s Hollywood epic that was based on it.'

This precious monument itself – as opposed to the text it bore – had been taken for granted for most of its history, and the exhibition provided the opportunity for its physical re-examination. Visitors were surprised to discover that the Stone's familiar black-and-white appearance was a modern phenomenon. Just as its original function had been forgotten, so too the nature of the Stone had been long in need of re-examination, as scientific examination showed:

Eric Miller
Conservation

'My first career was in insurance broking, spent largely in Africa. I left to go to art school in London, which was followed by a post-graduate training in conservation, and I joined the Museum in 1979.

For the *Cracking Codes* project I acted as liaison officer between the Conservation Department and the Progress Committee, which was formed to manage the preparation of the exhibition. My role was to co-ordinate the conservation of the 200 or so objects selected for it, which generally involved cleaning and stabilizing them, where necessary, for display. Additionally, I oversaw the imposition of special environmental conditions. These are routinely required for fragile objects that may be susceptible to vibration and high levels of light or atmospheric pollutants. Moreover, as fluctuations in humidity and temperature can be particularly damaging, the gallery was air-conditioned and it fell to me to carry out regular checks to see that safe conditions were maintained during the course of the exhibition.

I also worked with colleagues on the conservation and remounting of the stone objects and wall paintings. Included among these was the Rosetta Stone, which has been the subject of intense interest throughout the past 200 years. Strangely, the Rosetta Stone had never been properly regarded as an object in its own right. Although it is a stela that originally stood vertically, this function was ignored when it was mounted – tilted back – in the position reserved for displaying illuminated manuscripts. The character of the Stone – a grey and pink grano-diorite – had been obscured by protective coatings, which had discoloured to such a degree that the Stone appeared to be black on which was an inscription painted white. We removed these coatings and the white paint, along with a very thick layer of hand-grease, and the Stone was stood upright probably for the first time in 1,500 years.'

Human remains

As familiar from ancient Egypt as the Rosetta Stone are mummified funerary bodies. At the same time that the exhibition on the Rosetta Stone was revealing so many new insights, the Museum's permanent display of mummies was being brought up to date in the new Roxie Walker Galleries of Egyptian Funerary Archaeology. Nowadays, much greater attention is paid by museums to the way we display human remains. As well as being an extraordinary source of scientific or historical knowledge, the bodies of dead human beings are also emotional catalysts, and need to be treated with the dignity appropriate for a society that recognizes the ethical importance of respect for all other human beings.

The two Roxie Walker galleries prompted new research and provided a way of presenting the results to a wide audience. Several of the mummies were taken to London hospitals to be CAT-scanned, a totally non-invasive technique of looking within the wrappings which has provided important clues to the ages of the individuals at death, the state of their health, and the methods used to embalm them. Collaboration with the Museum's own Department of Scientific Research yielded an impressive range of data, notably identification of the timbers used by the ancient craftsmen to make coffins, furniture, statuettes and models for the tomb. This has in turn thrown light on ancient trading contacts and technological procedures.

John Taylor
Egyptian Antiquities

'I believe strongly that a museum should never stand still. Its collections are, or should be, an inexhaustible resource for expanding our understanding of the past, and the main means of stimulating that growth of knowledge is through research. Investigation of ancient remains, whether in the field, in the study or in the laboratory, is constantly changing our perception of the objects in the Museum's collections and revealing previously unknown evidence. The creation of a new permanent gallery provides an excellent opportunity to communicate the results of research to the general public in an accessible way. Finding an appropriate framework for the display of large areas of the collections is a challenge, and the curator must co-ordinate the work of many specialists, bringing different research strands into focus, while at the same time responding to unexpected questions that open up new avenues of investigation.

Even the most familiar exhibits can have new stories to tell. In the Roxie Walker Galleries a major aim was to contextualize the material – to present burial assemblages as coherent groups. A crucial preliminary step was to study archival material in order to ascertain the acquisition details and history of the groups of objects selected for display. This resulted in the recovery of hitherto underused data on their archaeological contexts, not only enabling the dating of particular pieces to be defined with greater precision, but also revealing previously unsuspected relationships between objects that shared a common provenance. As a result, the imposing gilded mummy-cases of a high-ranking woman named Henutmehyt (c. 1250 BC) can now be seen together with her funerary statuettes, amulets and food offerings, and with a sheet of papyrus containing funerary texts for the same lady – a rare and unusual piece that was identified after a sojourn of 90 years in another museum and was generously loaned for inclusion in the new display. A series of assemblages such as this, spanning 3,000 years of Egyptian history, is of far greater value as a didactic tool than the individual components displayed in isolation, and the sense of having helped to give back a voice to some of these mute objects after the lapse of so many centuries is one of the most rewarding aspects of the curator's job.'

As we already saw in Chapter 2, exhibitions are often accompanied by the publication of a book. To mark the opening of the Roxie Walker Galleries, British Museum Press produced a book aimed specifically at children. Why another children's book about mummies? The editor relates how the book developed:

Carolyn Jones
British Museum Press

'I had worked for years in educational publishing so, when a volunteer was needed to develop children's information books for the Museum, I had my hand up before you could say 'Hornedjitef'. Children's publishing is highly

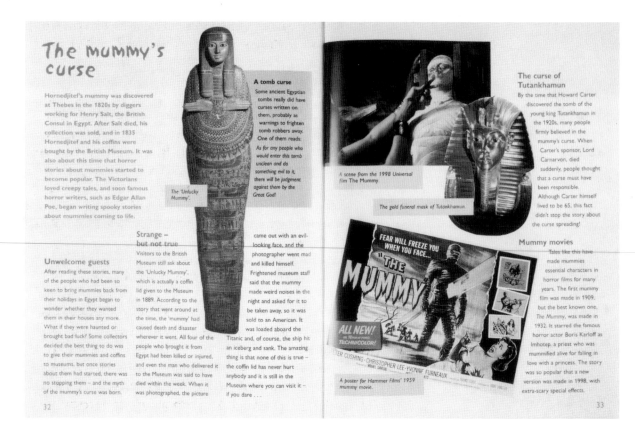

Pages from Delia Pemberton's *Egyptian Mummies* book.

competitive, and budgets are small. It's also a challenge to produce authoritative and lively material in a short, accessible format. The editor has to balance all the various requirements and stitch together different people's input without the seams showing – good editing is invisible. Working with an author and designer to realize an idea and produce a successful book can be a tremendously creative and satisfying experience. I've learned a few surprising things, and I've met some memorable characters – on both sides of the display-case glass.

Kids' books on mummies are legion, so how could we make ours fresh and different? Our author Delia Pemberton [see p. 93] had the brilliant idea of focusing on seven individual mummies. The book could explore all the different aspects of mummification through the characters of Hornedjitef and friends. More important, the seven were real individuals whose lives, jobs, hobbies and, in some cases, diseases could be described. Hornedjitef's shiny golden mask became a sort of mascot, radiating calm as our schedule counted down and deadlines loomed.

Finding unusual pictures of mummies became an obsession. We located images of nineteenth-century unwrappings, as well as the latest in CAT scans and X-rays. Could we obtain an ultrasound scan? Yes. Could we track down the one archaeologist who possessed a photo of the ibis galleries at Saqqara? Yes. Could we get a movie still from the 1932 Bela Lugosi classic? No – but we got a cracking poster for the 1959 Hammer horror flick. Some of us know better now, but we felt we had to include the 'curse of the mummy' material because evil mummies are so often the villains in books, comics and films. Sorry, Hornedjitef.'

Egypt's dry air contributes to the preservation of organic remains, whereas in damp climates like Britain they decay quickly. But, occasionally, a particular set of circumstances occurs in waterlogged deposits like peat bogs and the decomposition of soft body tissues is arrested due to the low temperature and lack of oxygen. At various times in the past people have been killed for punitive or religious reasons and their bodies thrown into bogs. When one such bog body was discovered at Lindow Moss in Cheshire, the coroner became involved because it was not immediately clear that it was an ancient body:

Ian Stead
formerly Prehistory and Early Europe

'Alerted by a telephone call requesting help with conservation, Museum conservator Sherif Omar and I travelled to Wilmslow on 7 August 1984, but arrived too late to see the body at Lindow Moss. It had already been boxed and removed to the mortuary at Macclesfield District General Hospital. Over the next few days the box was opened twice by the coroner's advisers, but after discussions with the excavators, landowners, police and coroner it was decided that all further excavation should take place at The British Museum. However, before the box could be moved the coroner had to be certain

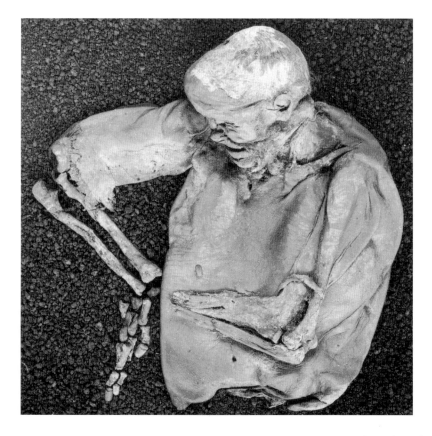

An ultra-violet photograph of the bog body from Lindow Moss. The garrott can just be made out to the rear of the neck, on the right.

beyond any shadow of doubt that the find was indeed ancient: he decided to keep the remains until a Carbon 14 date had been produced.'

Its eventual removal to the Museum was followed by a detailed programme of scientific investigation which has established the body's gender and date (male, first century AD), and how he died (probably knocked unconscious, garotted and throat slit), reconstructed his physique, examined him for disease and health (some worms), and re-created his environment and diet. Lindow Man is now one of the most well-known exhibits in the Museum.

Don Brothwell
University of York

'So what can we say about the last meal of Lindow Man? He had far fewer remains in his alimentary tract than the Grabaulle or Tollund individuals, and one should really refer to a snack rather than a full-blown meal. Was this in the form of conventional prisoners' fare – 'bread and water', or a gruel? The carbonized fragments might argue the case for a slightly charred bread, but of course the gruel pot could have been scorched! The probable absence of rye is not surprising, as it was not a common cereal in prehistoric Britain.

Compared with the food residue studied in Danish bog bodies, relatively few species are represented in Lindow Man, and a number of these are very likely to be accidental. The plant food debris in Lindow Man also seems to be finer in terms of fragment size. Moreover, while the Grabaulle 'muesli' contained over 60 plant species, and the Borre fen man made do on non-cereal wild and weed species, there seems to be nothing special about Lindow Man's repast except its simplicity. It was also high in fibre, so he would not have suffered from constipation or diverticulitis.

Mistletoe has been associated with Christmas festivities in Britain for many decades, and is claimed by some to have associations extending back to rituals of millennia ago. The Druids, for example, about whom, admittedly, much that is highly dubious has been written, are said to have used mistletoe in their religious ceremonies ... Tantalizing, though limited, evidence of this plant was found in Lindow Man's gut in the form of pollen grains (no seeds from the berries were noted), and small numbers of these were found in the intestinal tract. Where did this mistletoe pollen come from?'

Craft and technology

A special feature of The British Museum is that the staff includes a number of scientists who carry out detailed examinations of the composition of objects and clarify how they were produced. A range of scientific techniques is used to cast new light on the objects – where and how they were made, identifying fakes and so on.

Through investigating the Museum's collection of medieval enamel, which is the decoration produced by fusing coloured glass to jewellery

Ian Freestone using the scanning
electron microscope (SEM).

Ian Freestone
Scientific Research

and other metalwork, the techniques and practices of medieval craftsmen
have been revealed.

'Enamel intrigues me both for its beauty and for the skill involved in its
production. The temperatures involved in enamelling are not so different from
those of volcanic lava, which I worked on as a geologist early in my career. My
particular interest is in the glass itself.

Our work on enamel runs in parallel to that of the curators who are
preparing the catalogues of the Museum's medieval collections. I discuss with
them the best objects to examine, and where samples may be taken. I remove
tiny fragments of glass from previously damaged enamels and analyse them in
the scanning electron microscope. This tells me what the glasses are made of,
but to understand what this means, I need a lot of background information. I
need to know how the composition of ordinary vessel glass changed with
time, and from place to place. It has been possible to fill some of the gaps in
our knowledge through a project we set up on Byzantine glass-making, which
involved working with archaeologists and sampling collections in Jerusalem.
We have found that the medieval craftsmen re-used old glass, particularly
tesserae taken from Roman mosaics that had been made a thousand years
earlier. Some Celtic red enamel was even made using old metallurgical slag.

Perhaps most surprising is the finding that Byzantine craftsmen also used old, recycled glass for enamels, even though they had a thriving glass industry of their own.

When this work first began, it was hoped that each workshop used glasses of different composition, and that we would be able to say where the enamels were made. However, it is unlikely that anyone would make this suggestion today because we have shown that the colours that were used depended on recycling. In this way we have had some influence on the way people think about the objects and the people who made them.'

Another aspect of science at the Museum lies in its collections. It is not widely known that The British Museum has one of the finest collections of early European scientific instruments in the world, consisting of instruments used for telling the time (such as astrolabes, sundials and nocturnals), for surveying and for gunnery.

Silke Ackermann

Medieval and Modern Europe

'I am fascinated by European scientific instruments before 1600 for all sorts of reasons: the beautiful craftsmanship, the sophistication of the devices, the enormous amount of historical information contained on them – the list is endless. I particularly like to make a wider audience, both adults and children, aware of their existence and let them participate in the excitement I feel when I am handling these objects.

The research on scientific instruments in general is still in its infancy, and we seek every opportunity to discuss objects with colleagues from far and wide. Such an opportunity arose when four European museums (The British Museum, the Museum of the History of Science in Oxford, the Museo di Storia della Scienza in Florence and the Museum Boerhaave in Leiden) combined their efforts to compile an online catalogue of European instruments before 1600. The project, which was funded by the European Community, is called EPACT, which is not an acronym but a term indicating a particular feature used to calculate Easter. Epact tables are often found on the instruments in the catalogue. Obviously, the word also has a nice ring of E(lectronic) pact or E(uropean) pact – all of which it was. My role was to write the catalogue descriptions of the instruments in our collections and supply supportive material on makers, types of instrument, places and so on, and to supervise photography. We are all very pleased with the result, which offers material for everybody, no matter how deeply they want to delve into the subject: from brief descriptions to full-length catalogue entries, accompanied by zoomable colour pictures in a user-friendly set-up. There is great interest in EPACT, and people are already using it for research purposes we had not even thought of.'

Collaborators from the four partner museums all contributed different skills.

Giles Hudson

Museum of the History of Science,
Oxford

'Life as a museum IT professional moves at a rather different pace from life as a curator – or so those of us in the IT business would like to think. While the artefacts that curators deal with may be thousands of years old and don't change much from year to year, or even century to century, information technology in this day and age is progressing so rapidly that it is often hard to keep up. This can make life interesting as a museum IT provider, especially when undertaking large international cataloguing projects like EPACT which last several years.

Hardware and software has to be provided for curators at the beginning of the project, yet three or four years down the line the same equipment must look state-of-the-art enough to engage the museum visitor viewing the fruits of the curators' labours. Often IT officers are required to be soothsayers as much as anything else, but that no doubt is all part of the challenge.

When we first started working on EPACT, the Internet had only just come into existence and was very limited in how it could display text and images. Nevertheless, we decided that it was the future and so prepared EPACT in a web-compatible format from the beginning. Luckily, this has meant that it is a straightforward process to make EPACT available on the Internet, as well as on dedicated computers in the collaborating museums. Also, when we set

A page of EPACT showing an astronomical compendium by Johann Anton Linden, dated 1596.

out, very few electronic catalogues of museum objects had been published. One of our main aims with EPACT was to prove to a somewhat sceptical scholarly community that an electronic catalogue of scientific instruments could be a valuable research tool. In order to do this, we included detailed technical descriptions of the instruments in addition to texts aimed at the general public.

Another key strategy was to provide very high-resolution images of all the instruments, on large monitors, since for scientific instruments from the medieval and Renaissance period it is often the complex engraving on the surface that is of most interest to the researcher. Computers provide an ideal means of revealing this surface detail and do so in a way that can be superior to viewing the object in the flesh – instruments can be photographed under studio lighting conditions that are impractical to arrange in study rooms. This strategy seems to have paid off. Not unexpectedly, one of the most important criteria by which EPACT is judged, by scholars and the general public alike, is the quality of the images.'

Even if the collection of scientific instruments is not widely known to the public, everyone knows that the Museum contains pottery collections from all over the world. The British Museum offers unique opportunities for an interdisciplinary approach to research.

David Gaimster
Medieval and Modern Europe

'My research for *German Stoneware 1200–1900: Archaeology and Cultural History* involved bringing together a range of archaeological, historical, iconographic and scientific sources of evidence and this interdisciplinary collaboration was the aspect I most enjoyed about the project.

First and foremost, I wanted to deal with the archaeological evidence and in particular the international distribution patterns which reflect the commercial success and social impact of German stoneware from the Middle Ages to the colonial period. Much of the information was collected during extensive field trips I made over a five-year period to the former Hanseatic cities of northern Germany, Poland, Sweden, Denmark, the Baltic states, Finland and Russia. For a year I was a visiting research fellow at the University of Lund in Sweden. My travels not only provided raw data, sometimes straight out of the ground, but also the opportunity to share in the excitement of all the new discoveries being made.

The study also drew heavily on contemporary documents and graphical sources, so I was a frequent visitor to the collection of sixteenth-century prints in the Department of Prints and Drawings, looking out for contemporary archives, paintings and print sources to provide the missing link between the object and its context. It was fascinating to examine in detail the fusion of printed design source and moulded relief technology. An extensive programme of scientific analysis was also undertaken by colleagues in the Department of Scientific Research in order to clarify questions of stoneware technology and provenance, particularly glazing and clay recipes. This led eventually to fruitful conversations about firing temperatures and decorative techniques with practising potters interested in the history of their own salt-glaze tradition. The wide-ranging nature of the project also meant straying beyond the British Museum's own collection of documentary stoneware vessels to draw on the fine art pieces of the Victoria & Albert Museum and the local archaeological finds held by the Museum of London. The feedback and new information coming from readers and colleagues since the book was published have been a source of great satisfaction.'

A special exhibition, *Pottery in the Making*, highlighted the cross-cultural perspective offered by the Museum's pottery collections and was complemented by the publication of a book, a process reflected on by its editor:

Nina Shandloff
British Museum Press

Pottery in the Making: Phil Rogers demonstrates in the gallery.

'I've always worked in publishing. Now I work with curators and other Museum staff who write books based on research or exhibitions. We discuss what they want to say and how they'd like to illustrate it, and I suggest an appropriate format. We then work out how much the book would cost to produce and how long it will take them to write. Once the author has delivered the text the actual production process begins, which involves editing, designing and proofing both text and illustrations. If the author has never written a book before, I may need to answer a lot of questions about the process. I also nag a lot, because it's my job to keep to deadlines and to budget. This can be particularly difficult when the curator is writing a book at the same time as setting up an exhibition, because it is essential that the catalogue is printed and available by the time the exhibition opens.

Pottery in the Making was one of the most satisfying projects I've ever been involved with at the Museum. It examined the working methods, raw materials and techniques of potters in over 30 different cultures and societies, ancient and modern, from around the world. I have always loved ceramics and I know a number of contemporary studio potters, so I was able to forge a connection between the disparate worlds of museum curators, scientists and makers. The result was a unique collaboration. The exhibition displayed nearly a thousand pieces, drawn from every department of the Museum, and we created an equally unusual book. Both were enhanced by the active participation of more than 20 world-class potters from around the country, who gave free demonstrations in the gallery every Saturday and inspired everyone to look for unexpected relationships. These demonstrations were incredibly popular with visitors of all ages and they provided a dynamic link between potters past and present.'

Art and sculpture in the modern period

The history of cultures is not only told by the greatest or most famous works. The curator of *A Noble Art: Amateur Artists and Drawing Masters c. 1600–1800* hoped to reflect another point of view in the exhibition.

Kim Sloan
Prints and Drawings

'I began by simply going through the boxes of drawings and watercolours by British artists, the collection of 35,000 works that I curate, looking for works which illuminated not just artistic, but also social and cultural history. When I had selected 500 items covering two centuries, I tried them out in cases in the gallery when it was between exhibitions. Keeping the works roughly in chronological order, I wanted to cover various themes and connections that had begun to surface during my research. I knew that Mrs Delany's flower mosaics would be one of the most visually attractive and popular parts of the exhibition so I displayed them prominently near the entrance, but surrounded with works that would place them in a wider context. My PhD thesis had explored the introduction of drawing to various types of educational establishments and I looked for a way to tell this story within the physical constraints of the cases. It was a challenge to keep in mind the themes as well as the visual impact of individual items and to avoid overcrowding. Eventually, I ended up with 200 works.

After organizing conservation and photography, there were only six months left to write the catalogue. I was able to make use of research from my thesis as well as dossiers on artists compiled by previous curators. For the rest, I turned to secondary sources and books and articles on obscure artists that I had collected over the years. This was supplemented by research in the Paul Mellon Centre, the British Library, the National Art Library and Print Room at the Victoria & Albert Museum, as well as the Print Room of the Royal Library at Windsor, where there is a large collection of works by royal amateurs. Curators in these institutions, friends and collectors with expertise in various areas were the source of some of the most useful tips, advice and information. Writing an extensive catalogue and thematic essays while carrying out normal curatorial duties meant working most weekends and evenings; once the text was delivered there was no time to breathe before the proofs started coming back, exhibition labels and information panels had to be written and the publicity machine set in gear. After various panics with the printers, the catalogue eventually arrived on time and has turned out to be a handsome publication, which we hope will have a long shelf-life.'

Passion flower by Mary Delany (1700–88), made of over 230 pieces of carefully cut paper.

As well as works of art on paper, the Museum has a number of works of modern (though not contemporary) sculpture. Among the European ivories, enamels, ceramics, glass and waxes is a collection of around 90 pieces of British portrait sculpture made between the mid seventeenth and late twentieth centuries. Although it includes works by major British artists such as Joseph Wilton, Joseph Nollekens, Sir Francis Chantrey and Elisabeth Frink in marble, bronze, stone, terracotta, plaster, porcelain and stoneware, the collection was little known. It has been brought to the attention of a wider public by the traditional means of a catalogue, which lists the works and discusses their history and technique.

Aileen Dawson
Medieval and Modern Europe

Plaster of Philip Henry, 4th Earl Stanhope, by R.J. Wyatt, when partly cleaned.

'However long a curator works in The British Museum (and I have been here nearly 25 years), it is likely that there are sections of the collections in his or her care to which they have not been able to devote specialized study. Even the specialists I encountered when I began this project were surprised to discover how many pieces we have. Most are not on public display, and are kept in offices and rooms all over the Museum, as they reflect the Museum's own history. It became my mission to bring these 'hidden treasures', in many ways the private collection of the Museum, to public attention.

Scholarly work could not even begin on some pieces until a programme of cleaning had revealed the work of art beneath the layers of grime. One or two busts had suffered terribly from the coal fires that were once used to heat offices, and were black from pollution. After cleaning, the works were recorded by the Museum's photographers. Moving the sculptures around the Museum for both conservation and photography involved considerable organization. I decided to show the pieces from four sides, to enable others to study their construction and the skill of the artist. Artists' signatures and dates had also to be included. Although this process was both time-consuming and expensive, reproducing the images makes the catalogue much more useful.

I was gratified to be able to put on display a number of pieces that may never before have been seen by the public. A magnificent marble bust of King George IV by Joseph Nollekens had been badly damaged in a firestorm during the Second World War. After extensive conservation it was fit for display, although still blackened as we had decided against using a new method of laser cleaning to remove the smoke stains. In this case, we thought, it should remain as part of the history of the bust.

My study covered nearly eight years and took me to many different archives, museums and country houses. I rediscovered the identity of several sitters and came upon fascinating insights into the history of other pieces. Although the project had to be fitted in with all my other tasks, the sense of satisfaction when it was completed was well worth the effort.'

The reputation of the Museum as a source of reliable information has been based in part on works such as this, and the notion of the 'British Museum catalogue' as a standard reference book is still valid today. These works take many years to complete and have proved very durable, some remaining in use for over 100 years.

Archaeology and fieldwork

The light that objects already in the Museum's collections can throw on other cultures is complemented by new discoveries of similar objects *in situ*. Modern archaeological methods demand considerable documentation of the context in which objects were found, and this can greatly advance our understanding of exactly how they were originally used, when they were made and sometimes what they were used for.

The British Museum conducts excavations and undertakes archaeological and ethnographic fieldwork in many countries all over the world, with an emphasis on the recording of information from Britain (see pp. 59, 76). Abroad, the Museum has been involved in recent years in excavations in Italy, Libya, Albania, Turkey, Syria, Jordan, Egypt, Sudan, Ethiopia, Oman, Turkmenistan and Pakistan. A long-term project in Jordan has been examining a multi-period settlement at Tell es-Saʿidiyeh.

Jonathan N. Tubb
Ancient Near East

'When I joined the Museum many years ago I was both a specialist in the archaeology of the Levant and also a field archaeologist with many years of excavation experience already under my belt. I love excavation work – the combination of mental judgment and manual skill, and sometimes just the overwhelming feeling of discovery. To walk on the floor of a house that no one has set foot on for 5,000 years is one of the most exhilarating experiences you can imagine. And yet, for me, excavation is merely a means to an end. For what I am most excited by is using the results of excavation to piece together the history of ancient peoples. It is a bit like searching for clues in a vast detective mystery, and if you are the detective, there is no substitute for running your own dig – to design a programme to answer the questions you want to have answered.

For me this opportunity came in 1985, when the Department of Antiquities of Jordan granted me a permit to excavate Tell es-Saʿidiyeh, a huge double mound (or tell), in the centre of the Jordan Valley. This place has been almost continuously occupied from the Chalcolithic period of the fourth millennium BC to the Early Islamic period. Now, after nine seasons of

The excavation at Tell es-Sa'idiyeh in Jordan.

exhausting work, often in blistering temperatures, the site has yielded up some of its secrets. By 2700 BC, it was already a large and prosperous city, boasting an extensive palace complex with areas set aside for the production of olive oil, wine and fine textiles.

The most remarkable discoveries, however, relate to the city of the twelfth century BC, for, quite unexpectedly, excavations uncovered evidence for a major Egyptian presence at the site at this time. Substantial Egyptian-style architecture, including a palace and an elaborate water system, have been found, along with a contemporary cemetery with graves showing Egyptian-style burial customs and containing Egyptian-style grave-goods.'

The excavation has involved several other Museum specialists, including an archaeobotanist who worked on the reconstruction of the vegetation in Early Bronze Age times. Analysis of tiny fragments of organic remains, which are then compared and contrasted with archaeobotanical and other environmental evidence from other periods, helps to build a picture of ancient human activity.

Caroline Cartwright
Scientific Research

'When people ask me what kind of environmental archaeology I specialize in and I reply 'charcoal and wood', I suspect they must think 'barbecues'! In a way, they are not wrong – charcoal found in prehistoric hearths does tell us much about the plant foods and firewood ancient people selected from the local environment. But there is much more to the story. Under the microscope these little black bits reveal an intricate, fascinating and beautiful cellular structure, whose variety takes everyone by surprise when first they see it. Each tree has its own 'blueprint' of cells. In order to identify the tree, I need to examine these microscopic aspects of charcoal or wood. Then begins the process of environmental reconstruction.

For a site such as Tell es-Saʿidiyeh in Jordan, firstly I need to know where the plant remains come from. If they are charcoal from a domestic hearth, kiln or bread oven, they are likely to be fuel. If the fragments come from architectural contexts, then they are probably building timber. Piece by piece, I unravel the types of activities that involved plants. For the Early Bronze Age, I can separate the human food such as fruits, pulses and cereals from the remains of animal fodder and crop processing. Building on that and the extensive list of trees identified from the charcoal, I am then able to reconstruct the natural vegetation around Tell es-Saʿidiyeh and deduce how it has been modified by cereal and orchard cultivation. Studies of present-day vegetation help to reconstruct this model. It is not surprising, therefore, that those little black bits are treated with more than passing respect!'

Tell es-Saʿidiyeh provides an example of how fieldwork of this type can have direct implications for the Museum itself, since the excavation formed one of the important sources for the Museum's new Gallery of the Ancient Levant, which opened in 1998. Here it has been possible to display many objects from the excavations at Tell es-Saʿidiyeh, and even to re-create one of the rooms of the Early Bronze Age palace.

Jonathan N. Tubb
Ancient Near East

'The excavations at Tell es-Saʿidiyeh have proved to be exceptionally rewarding, not only because of the academic results, which have made a major contribution to the archaeological history of Jordan, but also for the Museum itself. For Jordan is one of the few countries that allows, at the end of each season, a 'division' of excavated finds.

The last week of the dig is a hectic time – closing down the excavation areas, paying off the workers and dealing with the finds. Everything has to be recorded, conserved as much as possible, drawn and photographed. At the end of this process, all the finds are laid out on long tables divided into two groups – those I would like to have for The British Museum, and those to be retained by the Jordanians. Representatives of the Department of Antiquities arrive from Amman, and the division is inspected. If all is agreed, we start packing the Museum share for transit – usually using the local polystyrene tomato boxes! We are then in the hands of the shipping agents, and if all goes according to plan, about three weeks later the crates arrive at The British

Museum. The choice of objects is very much conditioned by the needs of the Museum. I try to fill gaps in the collections, and also to obtain pieces that can be displayed.

In the new gallery we have been able to reconstruct a tiny room, which seems to have been the 'scullery' in the Early Bronze Age palace. Here we had excavated the remains of a 'last supper', the jars, bowls, mugs, platters and flint knives used for a meal for 11 people. Many of the vessels contained charred leftover food such as olives, grapes, lentils, chickpeas and capers. They had all been cleared from the dining room ready for washing up, when a fire broke out that destroyed the entire palace complex.

The accurate recording of this wonderful deposit in the field allowed for its realistic rendering in the Museum, and this process of 'bringing the site to the showcase' has been, for me, one of the most satisfying ways of presenting archaeology to the public.'

The Museum also participates in contemporary fieldwork in countries as far apart as the United States, India and China, enriching the Museum's collections and displays as well as our understanding of other cultures. Although fieldwork is a research technique, it is experienced in an intensely personal way.

Henrietta Lidchi
Ethnography

'Fieldwork is one of the most challenging and compelling aspects of doing ethnography. Over the last few years I have travelled often to Arizona and New Mexico to study the history of the stone, shell and silver jewellery made by Native American jewellers of this region. My visits have been anything up to three months, and my interest has carried me over tens of thousands of miles, interviewing jewellers on and off reservation and collecting their work.

I usually travel to the Southwest during the summer, the hottest season, in time for the summer fairs and ceremonials where the artists are keen to sell their work, and, during the slow periods, to talk more fully about their lives.

Fieldwork is an assault on the senses, composed of sounds, visual images, and smell, and it repeatedly presents intellectual puzzles. The experience dwells in the mind and returns powerfully and periodically, long after I am re-immersed in The British Museum.

I remember, for instance, an especially charmed day I spent in 1997 with the late Owen Seumptewa, a great Hopi photographer, and Michael Kabotie, a Hopi jeweller and artist who is engaged in a dialogue about the relationship between Celtic and Hopi symbolism. We spent the best part of the day discussing a necklace that I was in the process of purchasing for the Museum. The design is based on Hopi forms that existed before the Spanish first entered the region in the sixteenth century. Michael's father, the well-known artist Fred Kabotie, was key to the development of Hopi jewellery in the 1930s and 40s, when returning veterans were taught the overlay technique that is used for the pendant and is now a characteristic Hopi style.

Usually, in this type of interview, I make notes, and sometimes also tape

Michael Kabotie (Hopi) in his former studio in Flagstaff, Arizona, 1997, holding the pendant bought by The British Museum. The pendant is now on display in the Chase Manhattan Gallery of North America.
Photograph by Owen Seumptewa.

record and take photographs. But this time Owen, an old friend of Michael's, did the photography, with magnificent results. The outcome of this one day is a necklace on show in the Chase Manhattan Gallery of North America, a set of superior archival photographs illustrating technique and design, and a record of the artist's perspective on his work. Years later, it provides a testimonial to how productive a collaboration between artist, photographer and curator can be.'

Much of the research undertaken in the Department of Scientific Research is designed to increase understanding of ancient technology. Although studying the objects in the collection can provide many answers, it is also valuable to go to the places where the technologies were, or still are, practised.

Paul Craddock
Scientific Research

'I have always been fascinated by the hows rather than the whys of antiquity. Take brass, the ubiquitous alloy of copper and zinc. Analysis shows that many of the Museum's bronzes are in fact brass. That is surprising enough, but how did people make the copper and zinc in the first place? Smelting copper from its ores is not too difficult, but zinc is a different matter. At the usual smelting temperature zinc is a highly reactive gas and has to be condensed in special

apparatus. Old Indian alchemy books spoke of distillation processes for zinc, and I had heard mining engineers' tales of old heaps of retorts at a place called Zawar in northern India. So there we went and excavated, uncovering intact furnaces still bearing their last load of retorts, placed there over half a millennium earlier.

The earliest high-temperature distillation process in the world ended there about two centuries ago, but while studying the Indian technique I heard rumours of a very different zinc distillation process. Although this had long been thought to be defunct, in fact it survived in a remote western region of China. After years spent excavating long-dead remains I just had to go and see this process at work.

This was easier said than done. Modern China does not wish to present itself as a technical backwater, and the local officials were suspicious of our real purpose for wanting to see the zinc smelters. However, I made it. The smelters were wonderful, belching flames and smoke. The freshly smelted zinc was refined in a wok over a fire by stirring in a mixture of old plastic bags and rubber shoes! We established that this was indeed a truly indigenous Chinese method, made our notes, took photographs and video film and, by a combination of strength and persuasion at the airports, even managed to bring an 18-kg, metre-tall retort back in my luggage for the Museum's collection. This unusual item, a vital document of the diversity of human technical ingenuity, has since been used in a temporary exhibition.'

Bringing back the retort: a retort from Guizhou, China, starts its journey to The British Museum on Paul Craddock's shoulder.

In addition to its work in the rest of the world, the Museum has a significant responsibility in relation to the archaeology of Britain. As well as taking part in excavations itself, the Museum has responsibility for important archaeological objects found by chance or by people using metal detectors. Alongside the statutory provisions of the 1997 Treasure Act (see p. 76), the British Museum is developing a voluntary scheme in collaboration with other museums and archaeological bodies in order to preserve information about the many thousands of objects found every year by metal detectorists and others.

Roger Bland
Coins and Medals

'I have had a lifelong interest in Roman coins and for many years studied hoards of Roman coins found in this country. Some were declared to be treasure trove and so had legal protection; however, many were not and their fate was uncertain. For years archaeologists had been pressing for something to be done about this and in 1994 I was seconded to the Government to advise on improving the law. The new Treasure Act improved the situation but

A very rare decorated lynch pin, possibly from an Iron Age chariot, recently found near Winchester by Kevan Halls and reported through Sally Worrell, the Finds Liaison Officer for Hampshire, under the Portable Antiquities scheme. It has now been acquired by Winchester Museums Service.

the great majority of archaeological objects people find are still not covered by it. A recent survey estimated that metal detector users might find as many as 400,000 archaeological objects a year and that only a few of these were recorded because it wasn't the job of museums or archaeological services to do this work. As a result, a great amount of information about our past was just going to waste.

To complement the Treasure Act the Government agreed to fund a series of five pilot schemes around the country to promote the voluntary recording of all archaeological finds and The British Museum funded a sixth post. My job has been to get these pilot schemes off the ground and to prepare for a national network of finds liaison officers. In 1999 the original finds liaison officers were joined by a further six, paid for by the Heritage Lottery Fund. We have established a website (http://www.finds.org.uk) and are working on a lottery bid for a further 29 posts, which would enable us to provide a service across the whole of England and Wales.

There is no doubt that there is a great need for such a service. The finds liaison officers have won rapid acceptance from finders – who have recorded more than 34,000 objects during their first two years – and the scheme has also been widely welcomed by archaeologists and museums. Archaeologists in this country have not always been very good at explaining what they do to the public and the finds liaison officers are doing a great deal to raise public awareness about our archaeological heritage.'

Many different organizations are partners in the scheme and this number will increase if it becomes national. But its success in recording information is matched by its educational value, both in and out of school, for all sorts of people. The finds liaison officer for the West Midlands works with a number of museums throughout the region, recording chance archaeological finds made by people while metal detecting, gardening, walking their dogs over fields, playing on the school field or farming.

Angie Bolton
Birmingham Museum and Art Gallery

'Since most finds are discovered by metal detectorists, I attend metal detecting clubs in the evenings. These meetings are often lively occasions as people exchange ideas about their finds. My job is to encourage people to record them. The number of people who trust me with their finds is increasing, and I feel a sense of achievement that metal detectorists and archaeologists are now working together. Metal detectorist Bob Baldock recently commented in a local newspaper that the recording scheme is 'the best thing that ever happened to metal detecting'. He went on to say 'there was a time when archaeologists would not even speak to metal detecting enthusiasts, but attitudes are changing now.'

As most people work during the day it can be inconvenient for them to bring their finds into museums and this is why I attend the clubs. I collect the finds at one meeting, identify them and return them at the next meeting. Clive Kibblewhite, writing about his detecting club in Redditch, comments:

'All members … welcome this identification procedure. Finds are out of the owners' hands for only a month and everybody learns a lot.'

The objects I record are made of metal, pottery, glass and stone. However, not everyone knows what worked stone looks like and so, by using a handling collection of prehistoric flint tools and waste flakes, I try to teach people how to identify worked flint. There is nothing more satisfying than when someone you taught shows you their first fragment of worked flint for recording.

To encourage people to record their finds we have held exhibitions of metal-detected finds. These have proved popular with the metal detector users who lend their finds and also with children. They are encouraged to look in their gardens and local communities and become aware of the diversity of finds in their vicinity. Children are an important source of information and I organize a very worthwhile activity in schools, which involves volunteers playing the parts of Boudicca, a Roman soldier called Gauisis, a metal detectorist, an archaeologist and a dog-walker. We investigate what happens to the body and clothes of Boudicca or Gauisis when they die, and imagine what the archaeologist, the metal detectorist or dog-walker might discover. I try to encourage these children to think of a museum or archaeologist when they come across finds by chance and to become aware of what these discoveries can tell us about local history.

As well as meeting a huge variety of interesting people, I must be one of the few archaeologists to handle such a large number of archaeological finds. I identify and record artefacts from the prehistoric periods, right through to very recent history. Each find was owned and used by someone from history, and I may be only the second person to touch that object after the finder. Who used this find? How was the pot broken? How long did it take to make this flint axe? How old is this find? These questions and many more are asked by myself, finders, archaeologists, children and local communities, and I have the privileged position of helping to discover some of the answers by recording the finds.'

Angie Bolton (left) at a recent Local History Roadshow at Nuneaton Museum and Art Gallery.

The task of understanding our past and archaeology has come even closer to home with the new development works for the Great Court project over the past few years. The deep excavations and historic nature of the site have awoken interest in the Museum's own history and warranted its own site archaeologist. As with any other building development, the planning process requires evaluation of the archaeological potential of the site, and so a strategy to record anything that might be uncovered was developed in liaison with English Heritage and archaeological and site contractors.

Left The 300,000-year-old hand-axe excavated during the construction of the Great Court.

Opposite View of the East Lawn excavations from the Museum's East Wing, October 1997.

Tony Spence
Prehistory and Early Europe

'I have always had an interest in fieldwork, particularly excavation, and thus jumped at the chance to become involved in the Great Court and Forecourt redevelopment as an archaeologist.

We began to examine the areas affected by the building programme in May 1996, usually by looking down the trenches that the contractors were digging. In autumn 1998 we were able to examine the whole of the area around the Round Reading Room, which showed us the huge extent of the Smirke building programme of 1823–56. This had completely removed all traces of the gardens of Montagu House, but produced a mass of pottery, clay pipes and other largely eighteenth-century material from soil brought into the site to create a garden within this quadrangle. For me, the highlight of the archaeology in this area was when I picked up a hand-axe, some 300,000 years old, from the gravel that lies underneath all of Bloomsbury – certainly the oldest object I've ever found.

Most of our fieldwork has been in the Forecourt of the Museum, where Montagu House ran down to Great Russell Street. We have mounted four separate excavations here, two run entirely in-house. The three trenches across the East Wing and one in the south-west corner have shown rather more changes to the building layout than the three sets of plans show us, but I am working through the Museum archives uncovering many details to 'flesh out' the story.'

As well as staff from the Museum's curatorial departments, members of the photography and education services and central archives have also participated in the Great Court project. Long before the excavations started, a determined collaborative search of the archives began to reveal evidence of likely finds beneath the surface.

Christopher Date
Archives

'For fifteen years I have had the challenging task of helping to manage the records produced by the British Museum during the course of its daily activities. With records going back at least 250 years, there is a vast amount of material to look after and, despite the electronic age, this is growing by the day. As these are public records (in fact, part of the National Archive), public

access is a priority. Visitors come to our Students' Room to examine anything from a mid-eighteenth-century manuscript to a modern photograph while researching a whole range of Museum-related subjects.

Our aim is to maintain a lasting record of the Museum. Any changes to the building or on-site excavations are recorded with the help of photographs, video and computer-generated plans. Although we knew that Montagu House originally covered part of this area, the position was uncertain. However, from plans and drawings, some of the earliest photographs of the Museum and a series of detailed contemporary reports from surveyors, builders and Museum staff, Tony was able to plot not only the exact location of the old Museum building but also the depth of the foundations. This successful excavation and fieldwork project has produced some interesting object finds and yet more material for the Museum's expanding archives.'

CHAPTER 4

Curating

Other chapters in this book describe how the objects in the British Museum's collections are exhibited in London and museums at home and abroad, studied by scholars and scientists, enjoyed by children and collectors, and put on the Internet. But none of this can take place unless the collection is looked after properly. There are many facets to curatorship – ensuring the physical safety of objects, keeping records so that the context can be interpreted and understood, and also acquiring new material so that the collection remains up to date and can be used to do different things.

Making new acquisitions

Sometimes people are puzzled that a museum like The British Museum makes new acquisitions. Haven't they got enough already? And isn't most of it just rotting in basements? As we hope this book shows, objects that are not on display do play important functions, and certainly none of them are rotting away! Many cannot be displayed for long periods of time because they are vulnerable to light; nevertheless, everything that is not on display is available for members of the public or scholars to come and see, and these objects may also play an important role in a different way. For example, objects and other material from an excavation form a valuable part of the evidence for that excavation and it would be wrong to throw them away, although there may be little point in putting much of it on display. Again, the Museum has a collection of several hundred thousand coins; only about 10,000 are on display, but another 100,000 are consulted every year in the relevant Students' Room (see p. 98). The collection is similar to that of a national reference library such as the British Library, which is expected to have a copy of every book published (indeed, that is what the copyright laws of the country ensure), but nobody would require that every single book must be read or consulted each year. The comprehensive range and quality of the Museum's various collections are factors that help its curators to arrive at authoritative views and interpretations.

It may also happen that a particular sort of object was not acquired in the past, and it then becomes important to make selective acquisitions to ensure that certain parts of the world and their cultures are better represented. New archaeological discoveries are being made all the time, while throughout the world the westernization of many societies is leading to the disappearance of the types of objects that once symbolized and embodied them.

Changes in the cultural laws of many countries throughout the world mean that the new material acquired by the Museum is largely either contemporary or comes from Britain. The Museum does not wish to acquire objects that are not legitimately on sale, since to do so would be to encourage, either directly or indirectly, the looting and destruction of archaeological sites, whose integrity and proper excavation are vital if we are to extract the maximum amount of information from a diminishing resource.

The Museum does not anyway have the huge funds needed to participate frequently in the international market, but none the less every now and then, maybe only once or twice a decade, a spectacular opportunity arises.

Dyfri Williams
Greek and Roman Antiquities

‘In the summer of 1998 I was suddenly offered the chance to purchase for the Museum the Warren Cup, an extraordinary and most important Roman silver cup with challengingly explicit homoerotic scenes in relief. The sum needed to clinch the deal was £1.8 million. Although the Trustees quickly sanctioned the purchase, the Museum's annual budget for purchases is of the order of £0.5 million and it was already totally committed. The Museum was prepared to dig into some of its trust funds, and I needed to make serious assaults on a wide variety of external sources, ranging from private benefactors to more public sources.

Alongside this frantic but exciting work of fundraising went further research into the piece itself, especially its history. As a result, a great deal of detail was added to what was already presumed. It turned out that the first owner, E.P. Warren, an American who lived in Lewes in East Sussex, purchased the cup in 1911–12, when he was informed that it had been found at Bittir, some six miles south of Jerusalem. On his death in 1928 the cup passed to H.A. Thomas, whose attempt in 1953 to sell it in America was frustrated by a customs official who refused it entry to the US on the grounds that it was obscene. Thomas' widow succeeded in selling it to a British dealer soon after and in 1956 it was shown to the then Keeper of the Greek and Roman Department at The British Museum, Denys Haynes. Realizing its importance but also the problems of the subject-matter, Haynes decided to show it to Lord Crawford, an influential Trustee and a good friend. Lord Crawford, however, felt that, since the Chairman of the Trustees was the Archbishop of Canterbury, any proposal to purchase the cup would founder immediately.

The dealer made a number of further attempts to sell the cup in the

The 'Warren Cup', made in the early Roman empire (mid 1st century AD) and now on display in the Wolfson Gallery of Roman Antiquities.

following years. Indeed, in 1961 it was offered to the Fitzwilliam Museum in Cambridge, but despite the efforts of the Director and the Keeper of the department, the Syndics (Trustees) refused to purchase the cup and it passed into private hands.

The second chance to capture this cup and give it a permanent home in the public domain could not be missed. Nearly 12 months later, thanks to the generosity and support of several members of our department's international group of supporters, the Caryatids, namely Claude Hankes-Drielsma, Roy Lennox, Joan Weberman, and Richard and Josephine Kan, and with the aid of the Heritage Lottery Fund, the National Art Collections Fund, and The British Museum Society, the Warren Cup was acquired.

One of the British Museum's great tasks is to help visitors understand the multifarious cultures of the world, especially their origins and development. It is perhaps rare that an ancient object should challenge us so directly and explicitly across the centuries as the Warren Cup does. In doing so, however, it serves perhaps to reinforce the ongoing relevance of museums to the contemporary world.'

The legitimate opportunity to acquire something like this from antiquity is indeed rare, but this is not an issue with contemporary material. As described in Chapter 1, the Museum is collecting contemporary material, and celebrated this policy a few years ago with an exhibition called *Collecting the 20th Century*, covering the activities of six different departments. Works on paper from the twentieth century and beyond are now the fastest growing part of the collection of the Department of Prints and Drawings, since the establishment in 1975 of a post for a curator specifically charged with developing a modern acquisitions policy.

Frances Carey
Prints and Drawings

'One of the most exciting aspects of The British Museum is its involvement with contemporary art which is part of a continuing process of representing the whole history of mankind. The collection of the Department of Prints and Drawings now numbers some three million works on paper dating from 1450 to the present by artists of European cultural background, wherever in the world they may happen to live. Although the work of non-European artists is the responsibility of other departments – Ethnography, Oriental and Japanese Antiquities – we frequently discuss acquisitions together because artists so often move between places and cultural contexts. Much of the work is acquired through purchase or as gifts from the artists themselves, their dealers and collectors. Wherever possible, I and other colleagues try to visit studios and print workshops in order to gain a more complete picture of the artists' practice. Hope (Sufferance) in south London, for example, is one of the most important contemporary print workshops in Britain where several of our most notable recent acquisitions have been made, including 'Jake and Dinos' Disasters of War', the portfolio of 83 etchings inspired by Goya which the Chapman Brothers produced in 1999.

Plate from 'Jake and Dinos' Disasters of War', 1999, © Paragon Press and Jake and Dinos Chapman.

Exhibitions are a major part of what we do within the Museum and outside. Because works on paper are vulnerable to light they must not be displayed for too long and our programme has to change at regular intervals. Anyone may have direct access to whatever is not on view through the Students' Room [p. 98], which functions like a reference library where people can come for individual or group study. Many are artists who like to draw or just spend time examining a range of work of all periods. The evident pleasure our collection gives and the opportunity it provides for contact with artists are some of the greatest rewards of my job; here in front of our eyes we can observe the benefits of a great historic yet living collection.'

The Museum also makes a considerable effort to keep up collections of art from other cultures throughout the world. For example, it already has several hundred Shijō paintings from Japan, so why has it recently been buying more?

Tim Clark
Japanese Antiquities

'The Shijō school was the most influential new painting style to come out of Kyoto in the nineteenth century and fed into much of what we think of as modern Japanese painting in traditional style (Nihonga). It was revolutionary for the very familiarity of much of its subject-matter, often just 'ordinary' scenes of Kyoto and Osaka life, and for its light, lovely colour-wash style.

The biggest long-term project I am working on at the moment is a complete illustrated catalogue of the Museum's paintings, prints and illustrated books of the Shijō and related Maruyama schools. Such a catalogue does not yet exist for any major collection anywhere and I want to use it as the occasion to write about the development of public exhibitions and the art market in Japanese cities at the time. My recent purchases, then, are a classic example of trying to fill in gaps. Some of the gaps are large: we have no major paintings by Go Shun (1752–1811), founder of the school, and this gap will probably be expensive to fill. But I am constantly amazed by how cheap original paintings by some of the lesser known Shijō artists are; this is still not a subject that has received much attention in Japan itself, and we can sometimes fill important smaller gaps for just a few hundred pounds. We are buying works in all the traditional formats: hanging-scrolls, handscrolls, albums and even (now and then) pairs of large folding screens. Some are offered directly by collectors and dealers, but every time I go to Japan I try to visit a few new antique shops and scout around on my own.

The paintings spend most of their time rolled up inside wooden storage boxes, so the unrolling and re-rolling by the dealer is quite an enjoyable performance in its own right. When I look at a possible purchase lots of questions race through my mind. Why do I like it? Why is it special? Do we really need it? Is it genuine? What condition is it in? Is it the right price? Where will we find the money? Friendly Japanese scholars can then be pestered to help check signatures and seals and read any inscriptions. The final satisfaction is getting the painting cared for, if it needs it, in the Hirayama Conservation Studio at the Museum, and then putting it on public display in our Japanese galleries, alongside many old friends. '

Scenes from the Uzumasa Ox Festival and the Yasurai Festival, detail from a pair of handscrolls, ink and colour on paper, about 1800, by Kawamura Bumpō (1779–1821), with prefatory inscriptions by Ueda Akinari (1734–1809).

Famous objects

Famous objects already in the Museum's collection also need special attention, since the Museum has a duty to respond to the great public interest they attract. Only a few come into this category; they are always on display. Examples are the Portland Vase (p. 85), Lindow Man (p. 45), the Rosetta Stone (p. 40) and the Parthenon sculptures. Most people know that there is fierce debate about whether this world-renowned group of sculptures should be in Britain or Greece, but few are aware of the special trouble the Museum takes to ensure that they can be displayed and studied well. This does not mean that controversial questions should be avoided, but controversy should not overshadow the creative work of the Museum in making them accessible to an international audience.

Ian Jenkins
Greek and Roman Antiquities

'I look after the Greek sculpture in the Museum and that includes the sculptures of the Parthenon, often referred to as the Elgin Marbles. This can be one of the more difficult curatorial assignments as inevitably I get drawn into the controversy of restitution. Although from time to time that debate flares up, the Museum itself takes a long-term view – after all, the sculptures have been here for the best part of 200 years. During that time they have been loved and looked after by a succession of curators, whose job has been to make best sense of them for each generation and pass them on to the next.

In June 1998 the Museum opened two new galleries, generously funded by Barbara and the late Lawrence A. Fleischman. The galleries have two very clear aims: the first is to show millions of Museum visitors how the sculptures relate physically to the Parthenon in Athens. Among other ways, this is done with a computer-generated model that plays as a video. The second objective was to fulfil the Museum's long-standing commitment to promote understanding of the sculptures to the widest possible audience. A sound-guide is offered in seven languages and there is an audio accompaniment to a touch tour for visually impaired people. This is complemented by *Second Sight of the Parthenon Frieze*, a book presenting a tactile, pictorial synopsis of the frieze, and a touch model of the Parthenon, which were separately funded by William H. and Story John.

We enjoy these partnerships with private sponsors, who support and encourage our work but never try to direct it. Unfortunately, that was not the case in the 1930s when the financier and art dealer Lord Duveen funded a new gallery and put pressure on the Museum to clean the sculptures in a way that became highly controversial. Recently, the controversy flared up again and, amidst charges of conspiracy and cover-up, the Museum decided to hold a conference to look again at the issues. This took place on 30 November and 1 December 1999 and was a lively affair with some 300 delegates and a lot of media attention. It was, as one newspaper columnist put it, 'chaotic and risky', but it was also 'spirited' and 'a breath of fresh air'. The Museum was determined that it would be entirely open about events in the 1930s, and I assembled all the documentation I could find in the archives and sent it to everybody in advance of the conference. As an exercise in openness it worked, and we have now moved on to other challenges.

These include continuing research into the sculptures and improving and updating our various ways of sharing them with a worldwide audience. In addition, we have a special concern to maintain close relations with our professional colleagues in Greece, not least those at work on the Acropolis engaged in a long-term programme of conservation of the Parthenon itself and other monuments.

It is a privilege to be able to work with one of the greatest collections in the world, and the best way of acknowledging this privilege, and avoiding complacency, is by striving to communicate to as many people as possible why we care about these wonderful sculptures.'

Creating the Clothworkers' Centre for World Textiles

After the Great Court (see p. 105), the next major development for the Museum is the opening of the Study Centre. This is an ambitious scheme to convert an old Post Office building just 300 metres from the Museum (see p. 117) to provide enhanced storage and study facilities, and allow the public greater access to the Museum's collections and the processes by which they are conserved and researched. One aspect of this project is the creation of a textile centre uniting all the Museum's textiles in one place. This will mean that they can be looked after better and that people will be able to view them cross-culturally.

Many of the Museum's textiles have been collected in recent times from all over the world. Felts from Central Asia provide a good example of this activity.

Stephanie Bunn
Freelance anthropologist

'When the Department of Ethnography first discussed collecting Kyrgyz artefacts with me, I was requested to bring back small items that I could carry in my rucksack. My field research on felt yurts and felt-making among Kyrgyz nomadic herders showed me just what a challenge this would be, since Kyrgyz felts usually measure about 2m x 4m and weigh up to 10 kilos!

On my second visit, I had a more achievable brief and budget, enough for about eight felt carpets, which illustrated the different patterns, compositions, techniques and the variation of designs between different nomadic groups within Kyrgyzstan. A chance conversation with the director of the Kyrgyz-Canadian joint venture gold-mining company secured free transportation back to Britain of the felts collected. This effectively doubled the collecting budget.

On my return to Britain, the curator was so delighted that she suggested organizing an exhibition on the subject with me as anthropological adviser. I had a further period of fieldwork which enabled me to fill in gaps in the collection by acquiring some modern and tourist felts, and tools and raw

Kyrgyz floor felt (102 cm²), made in 1995–6 for sale to tourists.

materials to illustrate the making process. I also added to my collection of proverbs about felt to provide 'voices' within the exhibition, and my photographs of the felt-makers and felt-making to 'people' the display.

The Museum's collecting budget covered my expenses only. This meant that acquiring felts had to go hand-in-hand with my own field research. Yet this also enabled me – and at times pushed me – to extend my range of knowledge more than I might otherwise have done.

People's responses to selling their work to a museum affected me profoundly. It is unusual for Kyrgyz women to make felts to sell. The most elaborate felts – *shyrdaks* – are made for a daughter's wedding gift, and people traditionally keep these until they wear out. Otherwise, felts are traditionally made for gifts or for use. But everyone was tremendously proud to sell their work to a museum, especially The British Museum, which they had all heard of, and the money, at a time of extreme financial turmoil, was very welcome. This left me with a strong sense of my own responsibility to ensure that the felts did not just go into storage at the Museum, but were also displayed and seen. The *Striking Tents* exhibition was exactly what I hoped for.

Two Kyrgyz colleagues who had particularly helped me were able to come to the opening of the exhibition, and were strongly impressed that the display and documentation provided others with access to their culture. My biggest sadness was that the exhibition was not able to travel abroad and be seen more widely. My biggest joy was that something that began as a casual conversation at the beginning of field research turned into such a major project.'

Curators in The British Museum often have responsibility for very varied collections and even culturally and geographically diverse material. Developing links with specialists and institutions elsewhere provides

A felt-making workshop, organized in connection with the *Striking Tents* exhibition.

curators with valuable opportunities to complement work on their own 'patch'. *Striking Tents: Central Asian nomad felts from Kyrgyzstan*, the exhibition that ran from March to December 1997, was the first on the region in the Museum's history. It built on the series of textile displays held at the Museum from 1993 onwards, and also anticipated the kind of programme that it is hoped to develop in the Clothworkers' Centre for World Textiles (CCWT), part of the new Study Centre.

Sarah Posey
Ethnography

'I look after the artefacts in the Department of Ethnography from Europe, Central Asia and the Middle East, and have a special interest in textiles. I am part of the Museum-wide working party that is planning the CCWT, which will be made up of several elements. Visible storage will be added to the regular storage areas and will illustrate textile-making and -decorating techniques. Complete textiles, as well as partially completed samples, and the kinds of tools and raw materials Stephanie Bunn collected, will be on show to visitors. The display area will showcase recent acquisitions, support major exhibitions at the main Museum, or coincide with cultural festivals or curriculum-based projects. The vivid documentation Stephanie acquired – details of provenance and her stunning photographic archive – will be available for consultation in the research room, and there will be a host of activities aimed at a broad range of audiences.

My collaboration with Stephanie has been particularly rewarding and has significantly developed the Central Asian collections. For example, alongside the *Striking Tents* exhibition, Stephanie ran felt-making sessions, teaching people the extraordinary process of creating cloth from matted wool fibres. We organized a weekend seminar on traditional and contemporary felt-making, which was programmed with the help of the Crafts Council, with demonstrations and talks by craft makers. There were also story-telling sessions in the gallery – the tales from the nomads of Central Asia shedding light on the cultures from which the felts come. For me, one of the most exciting aspects of the CCWT-to-be is our aim to develop more and expanded hands-on events, demonstrations, lectures and seminars, in order to explore the processes and cultures behind the textiles.'

The Centre will contain material from many other places and times than contemporary Kyrgyzstan, indeed from all over the world. The task is considerable:

Helen Wolfe
Ethnography

'Problem (or perhaps I should say challenge): looking after 18,000 textiles belonging to seven curatorial departments at three sites across London (the main Bloomsbury site, the former Museum of Mankind in Burlington Gardens and the Department of Ethnography store at Orsman Road) with a storage system established in the 1970s and full to capacity.

Over 90 per cent of the Museum's textiles have been housed in the Department of Ethnography where I work. The variety of shapes, sizes and

Preparing the textile collections for new storage in the Clothworkers' Centre for World Textiles.

materials range from a small first-century BC Peruvian fragment exquisitely embroidered with figures and birds in vivid colours, to a quilted suit of horse armour decorated with colourful appliqué that was used in battle in Sudan at the end of the nineteenth century. The collections also include feather cloaks from Hawaii, mirrorwork blouses from India and raphia skirts from Central Africa. The list could go on ... and each textile has its own individual storage requirements.

Solution: the Clothworkers' Centre for World Textiles, where the combined textile collections will not only have a new specially designed and greatly improved storage facility but also enhanced public access through an ambitious programme of activities for groups as well as individual research.

My role: to co-ordinate planning of the CCWT facility and set up the Textile Preparation Project. The process: each textile is looked at and processed individually in preparation for the move, with information recorded on a data sheet to create a comprehensive record of storage requirements. Each textile is then packed and listed ready for moving to the CCWT. Flat textiles are rolled on to acid-free tubes to go straight into their new storage unit. Costume and delicate flat textiles will be stored in drawer units in the CCWT, so they have to be carefully padded and temporarily stored in boxes for the move. With the preparation and packing well under way, I am impatient to see the building work begin, and the exciting ideas become a reality.'

The Museum is turning to information technology to make the collection as accessible as possible, especially to those who are not able to visit the Centre itself. The aim is by the opening to photograph one-third of the entire textile collections – 6,000 pieces – and put the images on to a digitized database for the benefit of visitors, students, researchers, curators, writers, editors and readers of publications on the textile collections, and anyone with virtual access to the Museum via the Internet.

Brian Durrans
Ethnography

'Tuesday, 13 June 2000. Meeting at 4pm with colleagues to discuss the image-quality to aim for, the benefits the project will offer, how it will be staffed and managed, the implications it will have for other Museum strategies and objectives, how it might be funded, and the risks that might derail it. The workload will be heavy, involving a photographer and two museum assistants, and will take perhaps 18 months to complete before the start of the move out of the former Museum of Mankind in Burlington Gardens in London W1 towards the end of 2003. We aim to begin photography as soon as the textiles are processed for the Study Centre, in June or July 2001. For the past couple of years, our packing team have noted suitable pieces for photography so these can be easily retrieved once the project begins.

We'll need a digital camera, a way to link across from the image database to Merlin, the new collections database [see p. 83], someone to write or enhance the data accompanying the images, a way of putting the images and selected data on to the Internet, and the resources to make it all happen.'

Hoards and 'treasure'

The scheme for the recording of portable antiquities (see p. 60) sits alongside the legal protection of the past in this country. The antiquity laws in Britain are much less comprehensive than in many other countries, where generally speaking all archaeological objects are the property of the state. In Britain, or rather parts of Britain (since Scotland has its own legal provisions), only certain, important, finds have legal protection. The most significant consequence is that museums such as The British Museum are able to acquire new material for their collections, where it can be studied further and enjoyed by the public.

This legal protection was once provided by the medieval common law of Treasure Trove, which provided that any objects of gold and silver *which were buried with the intention of recovery* were the property of the monarch. The difficulty of proving the words in italics (and indeed the absurdity of arguing in a court of law today about someone's mind-set 2,000 years ago) led to an overhaul of the law and the passing of the 1997 Treasure Act (a summary of which can be found on the Internet at http://www.britarch.ac.uk/cba/potant15.html).

Jonathan Williams
Coins and Medals

'I specialize in Iron Age and Roman coins, and in 1997 a change in the law changed my life. The Treasure Act has extended the protection of the law to new categories of antiquities not covered by the old Treasure Trove system. It has doubled the number of hoards of ancient and medieval coins reported every year from England and Wales. Ninety-five per cent of hoards are found by one of the many thousands of metal detectorists who scour the countryside

in search of objects from the past. Finders report their finds to the local coroner, who then asks either The British Museum or a local museum to identify the coins and write a report on them. If a museum wants to buy any of them, then an inquest has to be held to see whether they qualify as treasure. Sometimes I have to appear in court and give my evidence under oath as an expert witness. The coins are then valued by an independent committee of experts. The acquiring museum has to come up with the full market value which is then paid to the finder by the Government. If nobody wants to buy the coins, they are usually returned to the finder.

Most large coin-hoards found in England come to The British Museum for study, and recording them takes about half my time as a curator. At any one time I may be dealing with 20 cases at different stages of the process. I send letters and e-mails to coroners, finders and civil servants to keep everyone in touch with the progress of work on a hoard. As The British Museum is the only place where work is done on finds from all round the country, I help to oversee the workings of the Treasure Act throughout England.

Iron Age and Roman coin-hoards form an indispensable, and growing, element in our knowledge of the ancient history of this country. My period covers about 500 years of British history during which Britain received many new cultural influences from the continent. Not the least of these was coinage itself, which first came into Britain about 150 BC and began to be made here about 80 BC. The Romans invaded Britain in AD 43 and brought with them their own coins which they used, buried and lost in huge quantities over the next four centuries, for us to recover today. There are records of about 2,000 Roman coin-hoards from Britain already, and they keep on coming. They seem set to do so for some time to come.'

Left The Alton, Hampshire Treasure, now on display in the Weston Gallery of Roman Britain. Deposited a few years before the Roman invasion of Britain, it included coins which gave us the correct name of a contemporary ruler in part of southern Britain, Tincomarus ('Big Fish').

Catherine Johns
Prehistory and Early Europe

There is sometimes a spectacular find among the 200 or so cases processed every year by the Museum. One such was the extraordinarily rich hoard of late Roman gold and silver coins, jewellery and plate originally deposited near Hoxne in Suffolk in the fifth century AD and discovered in 1992 by a man looking for a hammer he had lost in a field! Luckily, it qualified under the old law of Treasure Trove and was eventually acquired by the Museum for a massive £1.75 million. The discovery of the Hoxne hoard meant a lot of unexpected, though rewarding, work for the Museum.

'Treasures of gold and silver are interesting for much more than their obvious qualities of beauty and monetary value. As groups of possessions buried on a single occasion in the past, they can provide very significant archaeological information. The curators of the Romano-British collections regularly deal with treasures, and the discovery of a new one is not necessarily an occasion for excitement.

The late Roman treasure from Hoxne did stand out as exceptional from the first, however, because the finder had reported his discovery promptly and

Some of the gold bracelets from Hoxne, nesting in lumps of earth (right) and after their careful removal and cleaning (below).

enabled local archaeologists to conduct a professional emergency excavation on the site. When the Hoxne objects came to the Museum just two days after they were located, they were still, deliberately, only semi-excavated. The first task was to complete the field excavation by separating the coins, jewellery and silver utensils from their surrounding sandy soil and listing all of them in their context order, that is, the order in which they had been placed by the person who buried them in the fifth century AD. Cleaning and initial conservation were carried out at the same time.

The second phase was the compilation of the basic catalogue, numbering, measuring and describing each object in a rational order according to type. This order was retained for the Museum's accession register after the hoard was acquired, and it will be the same in the final published catalogue of the treasure. By the time of the legal process of the coroner's inquest, everything in the hoard had been photographed, many items were scientifically analysed, special storage trays had been made, and the design of the first public display, including information panels and labels, was ready.

Work on the treasure has continued since its acquisition in 1994. It has been on loan to Ipswich Museum, and is now permanently displayed in The British Museum. Scores of lectures have been given, and short introductory publications have appeared. Work for the definitive publication involves a great deal of planning, reading and, above all, thinking, as well as more photography, more study by archaeological scientists, drawings by highly skilled artists, and contributions from specialist scholars outside the Museum. A good catalogue should remain usable a century from now, and preparing one is a slow process. It is the publication of the catalogue, not the first sight of the treasure, that is an exciting moment.'

The hoard of around 200 objects and nearly 15,000 coins arrived at the Museum coated or embedded in lumps of soil. One of the most important tasks was its careful conservation, which was done in stages over a long period by Celestine Enderly and Simon Dove. The aim was to recover as much information as possible from the objects and attached soil to help to tell the story of their burial and original use or owners.

Simon Dove
Conservation

'Careful removal of soil with brushes and 'kebab' sticks revealed that the objects were made of gold or silver and highly decorated, some with gilding and inlays. The majority were in robust condition, but with much of the silver having patches of corrosion hiding surface detail. The few hollow silver objects were physically damaged; some were in many pieces.

The cleaning also revealed that many of the spoons were in nesting groups, as were some of the bracelets. The group of small bowls were stacked upside-down in a larger bowl with grass 'padding' between each bowl, and the top small bowl had patches of textile on the outer surface, possibly from a wrapping. This all suggested that the hoard had been carefully packed for burial.

Once cleaned and recorded, the second stage of conservation proceeded. This included removal of the layers of silver corrosion with mild chemicals and repairing broken pieces with adhesive so that they could be handled for study and displayed.

The most challenging work was the restoration of the four hollow 'statuette' pepper pots of finely moulded sheet silver, which were broken into several pieces. During assembly of the pieces with adhesive, it became clear that the bases contained a mechanism that had the dual function of filling and sprinkling the pepper. One mechanism was still in working order.'

After temporary display first in Bloomsbury and then in Ipswich Museum, the hoard is now on permanent view in the Weston Gallery of Roman Britain. But, at the same time that it is being enjoyed by the public, the long process of research continues.

Peter Guest
Bristol

'I was very pleased when the Museum suggested that I prepare the catalogue and write the report on the coins in the Hoxne Treasure. This is a once-in-a-lifetime opportunity and, although it has sometimes seemed a long and winding road, I have found it immensely rewarding.

The first task was to bring order to the many coins sitting in envelopes in a large heap in the Department of Coins and Medals. For over a year I sat at my desk slowly sorting the coins into different denominations and arranging them according to when they were made and the mints at which they were struck. In the end I counted 580 gold coins (*solidi*), 60 large silver coins (*miliarensia*) and 14,140 smaller silver coins known as *siliquae*. These are about the size of a new 5p piece and whenever I have difficulty sleeping I count *siliquae* rather than sheep!

Most of the coins were struck between AD 360 and 400, a very interesting time in our history when the Roman empire's grip on Britain was coming to an end. In fact, the latest coins are dated to AD 408, though there are only six of these in the entire Treasure (truly a numismatic needle in a haystack!). Two of these were struck for the usurper Constantine III who had been an official in Britain before deciding he should be emperor of Rome. In pursuing his ambitions Constantine III collected the last remaining units of the Roman army left in Britain and marched against his enemy's forces in Gaul. Ultimately, Constantine's usurpation failed and he was executed, but the consequences of his actions changed the history of Britain forever. Roman Britain soon became Anglo-Saxon England.

For me, the coins from the Hoxne Treasure bring the past to life and in the catalogue I included chapters that look at the Treasure from the perspective of fifth-century Britain. Because of this project we now have a better idea of why the Roman empire struck gold and silver coins (to keep the army happy and to fund civil wars), why the *siliquae* had each been 'clipped' around their edges (probably for high-quality silver to make more local copies of these coins) and why so many treasures of gold and silver objects were buried in

Britain at this time (we're still not too sure about this, although it almost certainly wasn't because of marauding Angles and Saxons). The careful study of the Hoxne Treasure shows how important archaeology is to understanding our past. It is a bright light in an otherwise dark age.'

Looking after prints and drawings

We have seen some aspects of how the Museum looks after the objects in its collection – how they are acquired, conserved, studied and classified, housed, published and displayed. It is an enormous task, and new techniques are always being developed and brought into use. Key elements in the work are conservation and documentation: keeping the objects in good condition and maintaining an accurate record of them. The conservation of works of art on paper is a delicate and skilled activity and, as well as making improvements to the environment in which they are kept, there is a regular need for exhibition and sometimes remedial work, which may bring surprise benefits.

Jenny Bescoby
Conservation

'A conservator's job is to work with curators and scientists to make sure that the objects on display and in store are in as good a condition as possible. Conservators usually specialize in a particular material; my expertise is in paper. As most of my time is spent on the collections of the Prints and Drawings Department, it means that not only do I have to have the precise practical skills for working on these objects, I also need a background knowledge of science and art history.

My day-to-day activity is studio-based; I am usually working on prints, drawings and watercolours, but sometimes on objects as diverse as pastel paintings, maps, posters, tracings, even cigarette and playing cards. I have worked on preparing a Michelangelo drawing for loan to America one week, and on a torn and dirty Victorian penny ballad sheet for the *Popular Print* exhibition the next. Sometimes objects need repair or cleaning. Technology in conservation has advanced and now many specialist techniques have been developed to avoid using strong chemicals. Our tools must also be very precise: a surgeon's scalpel or the finest sable watercolour brushes.

There are deadlines to be met for exhibition displays and loans to other museums, and there are always ongoing storage projects. A project we completed recently was to remove all the Rembrandt etchings (about 1,000) from their old dirty mounts. As the prints had been glued down for many years, it was very exciting to discover inscriptions and collectors' stamps which had been hidden from view. This was also an opportunity to collaborate with the Department of Scientific Research in recording the watermarks by use of X-radiography. It was immensely satisfying to see the etchings in their new mounts, back in the Students' Room and protected for the future. This is one of the most important aspects of our work.'

Melancholia, an engraving by Albrecht Dürer (1471–1528).

Maintaining records of the objects in the Museum's collections is a necessary if time-consuming activity. Since the earliest days, the Museum has kept paper inventories and listed every new acquisition in them. New technology offers a better way of keeping track of the collections and ultimately improving the public access to them.

For several years the Museum has run an IT collections management project, and it is proving of particular value in relation to prints and drawings.

Sheila O'Connell
Prints and Drawings

'I first worked at the Department of Prints and Drawings in the early 1980s and when I came back in 1989, the one inescapable change was the arrival of computers. At first there were only word-processors, but looming on the horizon was the huge project to create a database of the entire collection of more than three million prints and drawings.

Curators were very excited at the prospect of what would in effect be an extremely complex index to the collection, but we were also daunted by the amount of work involved. The database is not purely an academic exercise; it fulfils the Government's demands for proper auditing of public property, so we are not allowed to work at the steady pace at which traditional comprehensive British Museum catalogues are produced. A target of 600 entries a month was set at the start of the process. There is no time for thorough research on every print and drawing, but we are determined that what is entered is accurate as far as it goes. Some information is straightforward – dimensions, medium, location – but most is not. Sometimes there are yards of learned prose to be boiled down to fit into data fields; sometimes there is nothing to go on beyond a brief register entry made at the time of acquisition.

After nearly 10 years of work by curators, collections data staff and teams of volunteers (without whom we would not have been able to cope), we have

Tanya Szrajber working on the Museum's computer database.

a total of 61,000 entries on the prints and drawings databases. These include all the drawings in the collection and most of the twentieth-century prints. Next will come the earlier prints, from Dürer's *Melancholia* to Landseer's *Monarch of the Glen*. Every one will bring its own problems and will demand to be treated in a different way.'

The purpose of the collections documentation project is to produce a computerized catalogue of all the registered collections in The British Museum. Most computer records in the collections database are entered by specialized Collections Data Management staff, while curators are responsible for researching, updating and checking information and for creating new records for recent acquisitions. There must, of course, be close co-operation and mutual understanding between everyone involved.

Tanya Szrajber
Scientific Research

'I enjoy the combination of art history, which I studied academically, and the documentation of museum collections on computer – a relatively new and exciting discipline in the history of museum work. My responsibility is for standardization across the databases of all the curatorial departments, and for terminology control. This ensures that one computer system can be used to document any type of object, from almost any historical period or world culture, based on the fact that certain types of information are common to most objects: museum registration number, physical location, description, object name, dimensions, date or period, provenance, maker and so on.

Terminology control is essential if, for example, someone searching the databases for 'vessel' needs to call up all possible records, whether they describe sake-cups, bowls or drinking-horns. The requirements for the Department of Prints and Drawings presented a particular challenge since its collections are two-dimensional, whereas the others generally consist of three-dimensional, often archaeological, material. Thus the emphasis was more on artist, subject-matter and provenance rather than, say, material of manufacture or site details.

Another feature was the sheer size of the collection, which meant that the level of information recorded had to be sufficiently detailed to allow staff and visitors to make useful database searches, yet concise enough to make the project realistically viable. Working in close consultation with the Keeper, Antony Griffiths, and Sheila O'Connell, one of the curators, we considered several approaches before we agreed on a method. We decided to cover specific areas of the collection – British drawings, French drawings, etc. – rather than working by storage area or subject-matter (such as portraiture). We had to devise a subject classification that was simple enough to cater for the general user as well as a controlled list of artists' names, with basic biographical details. It is satisfying to see that this newly increased access to information has already provided many benefits to Museum staff and, via the Students' Room [see p. 98], to the public.'

Nigel Williams begins the process of dismantling the Portland Vase in 1989.

First aid

Accidents happen. Sometimes people make a deliberate attempt to damage things. One of the Museum's most important treasures, the rare and exquisite Roman glass named after its original owner as the Portland Vase, was smashed in an act of vandalism in 1845. The fragments were rapidly restored at the time and the vase returned to exhibition. However, it has been repaired again since, once in 1947 and then again, using modern techniques, in 1989. The conservator who conducted this process, who has since died, described how the vase, carefully bandaged with supporting blotting paper and plaster, was first taken apart and reassembled.

Nigel Williams
formerly Conservation

'Rather like a tooth being extracted, the first fragment was pulled away. Then the clamps were carefully undone, the paper rolled back and the exposed fragments lifted away one by one. As each fragment was removed it was numbered and placed in the appropriate position on the plan. The whole operation was very controlled: no rush, no collapse, no new breaks. By the end of the day the Vase lay in 189 pieces (not 200, as was originally thought).'

Everything was carefully cleaned and reassembled over a period of many weeks.

'The next stage was to replace all the missing areas with resin of a colour that matched the original. There are several very stable blue pigments available, but in order to obtain a true colour match some violet colour had also to be added, and these are notoriously unstable. After much searching and testing, a violet pigment used by a large firm of car manufacturers was found to be suitable.

All the remaining holes were backed with sheet dental wax, and the resin was slowly built up until each hole was a little over-filled. After a few hours the excess resin was wiped away with cotton buds and acetone. When each patch matched the contours of the Vase almost exactly it was left to harden completely ... When the resin was hard, the final shaping could be carried out using very fine polishing papers to avoid scratching the glass. Finally the resin was polished so as to appear similar to the original without being completely invisible.

After nine months' work, the Portland Vase was ready to be returned to permanent display, the conclusion of another episode in its eventful history.'

People have also tried to steal things. A theft of coins in 1849 was investi-

The Museum's 'burnt-out medal room' after the air raid of 10 May 1941. A letter written at the time by the Museum Secretary refers briefly and laconically to 'the bad time we had on Saturday night last'.

gated by one of the Museum's Trustees, Sir Robert Peel, the founder of the modern police force, but attempted thefts are thankfully rare. A former director, Sir David Wilson, recorded how in 12 years of his tenure only three items were stolen from public display, one a stone inscription that was prised from its mount on a crowded Sunday afternoon. The Museum employs more than 300 warders (see p. 105) to protect the collections in such circumstances, and they also carry out other functions including public safety. There are many security systems, such as alarms and CCTV, and the documentation of the collection means that if anything were ever stolen it would be very hard for anyone to sell it without it being recognized. Strangely enough, we decided we would not reveal full details of these security systems in this book.

The Museum has suffered disasters, such as in the Second World War when it was hit by a number of bombs. The Department of Coins and Medals was burnt to the ground by a fire-bomb in May 1941, but even though the collection had long since been moved to a place of safety, the sight of 'the burnt-out medal room' had a profound effect on visitors such as the distinguished archaeologist Sir Arthur Evans. Natural disasters are as yet unknown, but the Museum maintains 24-hour, 365-day-a-year care of its collections. Throughout the night the Museum is protected by the constant presence of security warders who make regular patrols. In addition, a duty curator is on site or on call in case of any problem. During the construction work for the Great Court Project the potential risk was greatly increased. If any threat to the collection arises, the duty officer is alerted by security staff from the Control Room. All activity is logged in the Incident Book:

John Curtis
Ancient Near East

'2am. The Control Room rang. Water penetration in two rooms. Rain had been persistent for the previous 12 hours but not heavy. Immediately obvious that the problem was serious. Water coming down the wall in many places where the galleries abut the east wall of the Great Court. Contractors contacted and asked to investigate urgently.

3am. Phoned Keeper of Department and warned that it might be necessary to bring in departmental staff. With warders then set about protecting cases with plastic sheeting, puddle pythons, etc.

5am. It was clear that we were fighting a losing battle. Decision taken to activate departmental cascade system, to bring in departmental staff. While waiting for their arrival, I started emptying cases, with great support from the security staff.

6am. Departmental staff arrive and take over.

7am. Return to Duty Flat.

N.B. The security staff were outstanding.'

Such incidents are rare. The fabric of the Museum is regularly maintained, but a problem can arise when, as with the Great Court, a new building is under construction on the same site. Luckily for most duty officers, a stint of duty is usually much less onerous, as for John Mack:

'The only thing of note was a fox seen at dawn going down Malet Street, over the pedestrian crossing and apparently into the Senate House of the University of London.'

CHAPTER 5

Visiting

The British Museum is the most visited museum in Britain, and one of the world's busiest. Because it has such a wide range of visitors it provides an increasingly diverse range of programmes, from the informal drop-in gallery tour to the academic conference or intensive course. The Museum has a variety of ways to help visitors with different learning styles and appetites to become more familiar with other cultures, and to see their own cultural roots in context.

En route for a morning gallery talk in the Egyptian galleries.

Guides and tours

Most visitors are from abroad and many of them come in large groups. Coach parties of tourists are often accompanied by tour guides who have received special training from the Museum's Education Department, on top of their Blue Badge Guide training. Other guides present the

Museum's regular daily programme of highlight tours, which attract couples, single visitors, or perhaps visitors from abroad on a repeat visit. Visitors can also choose to concentrate on a single culture by taking an 'eyeOpener' tour, led by a trained volunteer. The eyeOpener tours are a good example of the Museum learning from others, in this case from America, and particularly the expertise of two experienced American museum docent trainers. The tours are informal and deliberately not specialist. The guides enthusiastically introduce Islamic art, North America, ancient Egypt or Roman Britain.

Susan Harrison
Education

'EyeOpeners began as a pilot project in 1992 with a small group of willing volunteers who were trained to give introductory tours in the newly refurbished Hotung Gallery (Room 33). Now there are 100 guides who volunteer their time to provide eight different tours a day, seven days a week, covering most of the major areas of the Museum. The tours are free and available to anyone waiting at one of our meeting points. I joined as a guide and moved on, first to help in the office and then to manage the programme. My interests and experience lay in the medieval and Renaissance periods, but because of the nature of eyeOpeners, I have had the opportunity of working with collections and curators across the Museum. Luckily for me this has been in digestible stages! As well as the day-to-day running of the programme, my task is to ensure standards are maintained and to plan and initiate further development.

When creating a new tour I work closely with the relevant curatorial department and my colleagues in Education. Each tour is based on a number of objects, selected to illustrate major themes. Training courses last approximately eight weeks, are related to a specific tour and include instruction in technique as well as providing all the subject information required. They consist of gallery talks and lectures given by curators, and are held once a week in the early evening to enable people in full-time employment to participate. They then also have the added bonus of being in the Museum at night when gallery spaces are empty and exhibits are often lit to spectacular effect, taking on a very different appearance.

Within the guiding team we have a broad mix of ages, skills and experience. The common factors are volunteers' enthusiasm for their subject, their commitment to the Museum and their ability to communicate these passions to others. The aim of eyeOpeners is to give visitors an overview of a particular culture or period along with a general understanding of how to use the galleries. We hope this approach not only makes a visit enjoyable, but also encourages and inspires people to return. On

EyeOpener gallery tour in the Early Egypt Gallery, looking at 'Ginger'.

many occasions visitors have shown extraordinary stamina in moving from one tour to the next, trying to take in as many as physically possible in one day. 'Thank you for making it all come alive' was the parting remark from one American family recently, one of the many positive comments the guides receive, and which help to make our job worthwhile.'

Hazel Beale
Education

'I first discovered eyeOpener tours three years ago when I found that I could run across to The British Museum during my lunch break and fit in a different tour each day, covering the whole series in a week. Now I am still running across in my lunch times twice a month, as a fully fledged eyeOpener guide! I go round the office beforehand, saying 'Tour of Roman Britain about to commence in 15 minutes', and many lively discussions have taken place back in the office afterwards on different aspects of Roman life. The groups I take invariably enjoy the tour, and I get many appreciative comments afterwards. It has enormously increased my knowledge of history, and there are endless possibilities for the future.'

In the context of lifelong learning, it is important for visitors to feel at ease, free to ask questions and find out more, so that they can become more confident learners. The way this process works in a museum is not unlike an escalator, carrying learners step by step upwards from an eye-Opener or highlights tour to a gallery talk or lecture given by a curator, a freelance lecturer or a member of the Education Department, and then, firmly smitten, on to study days and courses. Ancient Egypt has been one of the most popular areas of the Museum since at least the 1830s and its galleries are the most intensively visited by schools, families and adults alike. The education officer responsible for this area is the author of numerous popular books on ancient Egypt, some of which have been translated into many languages.

George Hart
Education

'I started out at university obsessed with Homer and the Trojan War, but eventually the pharaohs triumphed and my postgraduate studies were in Egyptology. Following a teacher training course, I joined the British Museum's new Education Service in 1973. What were core duties then still form an integral part of my work now – communicating ancient Egyptian antiquities to schools and the general public through lectures and written resources. However, since then the Education Department has become much larger, more professional and of greater significance within the Museum. I also now co-ordinate the varied repertoire of gallery talks given by Museum staff and outside lecturers, and I also take part in this programme myself.

In a gallery talk I always try to let the objects remain the focal point and through them bring in history, religion or archaeology. In the case of the magnificent red granite lion in the Egyptian Sculpture Gallery (Room 4), I emphasize its importance as a work of art, but also the technology involved in carving it – then draw attention to the fact that it bore the name of

Tutankhamun (one of the few objects to survive that is not from his tomb). I also relate it to the history of the Museum's collection, by pointing out the name of Prudhoe on it – he was responsible for bringing it back from the Sudan in the 1830s.

Slide lectures range more widely over themes such as dynasties or archaeological sites, but I always try to forge a link with objects in The British Museum. I teach two courses on hieroglyphs each year for the Museum. It is very rewarding to see students of all ages relish the thrill of turning pictures into sounds, although it is a more daunting task to keep their interest when we move on to the complex grammar needed to translate texts. I also teach adult education courses on Egyptian religion, art and history, which means that I try to keep abreast of the most recent scholarly and popular literature.

George Hart teaching about Egyptian art.

I use my annual leave to keep in touch with ancient Egypt, the Levant and the ancient Mediterranean by accompanying British Museum Traveller tours and Swan Hellenic cruises as guest lecturer. It has been exciting to be involved with the Museum's own travel company over the past 10 years and to take Museum visitors to the original source of many of its collections. I find it immensely invigorating to work in such a diverse and dynamic department, which is at the cutting edge in enticing new audiences to take an interest in our collections, as well as meeting the expectations of our traditional supporters.'

Young visitors

Not only are the mummies irresistibly attractive to all ages, they are part of the national curriculum used in all English state schools. So it is not surprising that there is a long waiting-list to take part in sleepovers in the

Egyptian galleries, which are organized by the Young Friends of The British Museum.

Delia Pemberton
Freelance educator

'I have many different roles within the Museum: in the same week I might be giving lectures and gallery talks for adults, running workshops for children or developing educational resources. I also work outside the Museum, teaching in other museums, schools, adult education centres and universities, as well as writing books and articles about ancient Egypt for adults and children [see p. 44]. However, most people in the Museum know me as the person who gets children to 'mummify' each other with toilet paper!

A large part of my work involves organizing and presenting workshops and events for the Young Friends of The British Museum. As the junior branch of

The 'toilet-paper lady' in action.

The British Museum Friends, YFBM encourages young visitors to develop a sense of ownership and involvement with the Museum by participating in a wide range of activities such as drama and conservation workshops, behind-the-scenes sessions and site visits. My main responsibility is organizing and presenting the Sunday Club, a programme of fortnightly events held on Sunday mornings throughout the year, and aimed at providing a social space where Young Friends can meet each other and have fun exploring the Museum's collections. I also present workshops at sleepovers, when up to 300 children and adults participate in an evening of themed activities in the Museum before enjoying a midnight feast and settling down to sleep in the galleries. For me, the best part of my job is getting to know our young visitors and helping them realize they're an important part of the Museum community – and as long as they're happy, I really don't mind being known as the toilet-paper lady!'

The Sunday Club and sleepovers cater for a wide range of ages and abilities, so a lot of work has to go into planning workshop content and delivery. As well as having fun, Young Friends really want to learn about other cultures, so there are lots of hands-on activities to give them a feel of life in other times and places, such as preparing and eating Roman food, making and playing Viking board games or writing on papyrus in Egyptian hieroglyphs. Many of the best ideas come from the Young Friends themselves:

Lotte Johnson
Young Friend (age 11)

'I recently went to the Native American sleepover. It was great and I really enjoyed it. We did lots of activities including making dream-catchers. This was very tricky as you had to wind the string in a special order. My finished piece looked nothing like the professional ones on the wall but it was very enjoyable making them. Another activity that I particularly liked was building a longhouse. Two men had brought long and short canes of wood and rubber bands. This simple equipment was soon transformed into an amazing structure of a longhouse. Our whole group fitted into it, as well as our parents! I also enjoyed the soap sculpting. We all chose an object from the Native American gallery and were given a bar of soap to carve it from. I did a stone cat with patterns engraved all over it. The best activity had to be story-telling, the man involved everyone in the story, getting us to join in with phrases and communicating really well. A really exciting prospect of the sleep-over was that our activities finished so late that bedtime was at midnight! The sleepovers are a fantastic idea and I hope I can go to the next one.'

Thomas Gardner
Young Friend (age 9)

'I am just recovering from the exhausting but tremendous fun Greek and Roman sleepover. My group first did mask-making. I did the gorgon Medusa. It was excellent. I don't think it would have been so good, if we hadn't had the person who helped us. Next Parthenon building. This was my favourite. With mere bamboo sticks and elastic bands we created a wonder. After that we listened to story-telling. We looked at the statues and then made some busts. I don't think mine looked too good though! In the morning we participated in a drama workshop. That also was brill. We did lots of exercises to make our acting better. Last we went to collect prizes – I did not get one.'

Families and children outside school are catered for by the Families Officer in the Education Department through a programme developed with funding from SmithKline Beecham. This is one of many areas of sponsorship, secured with The British Museum Development Trust, which have enabled the public work of the Museum to develop rapidly in the past five years. Recent family programmes have included dramatic re-tellings of the Trojan War in the Greek galleries and the epic Gilgamesh in the Ancient Near Eastern basement galleries, celebrations of Chinese New Year and the Eid Festival. At either end of the Hotung Gallery are spaces for performance which have seen Indian dancers, Chinese pup-pets, Peking opera, calligraphers and story-tellers. Family activity trails are always available, and the Ford Centre for Young Visitors in the Great Court can be used by families to eat lunch when it is not in use by schools.

Spreading the word

The Education Department has recently nearly trebled in size and now consists of over 40 people, including archaeologists and art historians, teachers and librarians, classicists, video-makers and multimedia authors, administrators and technicians, an anthropologist and a scien-tist as well as education officers dealing with access, primary education and lifelong learning.

John Reeve
Education

'I started out as a teacher in school and adult education and then became a museum educator. I am now Head of Education, which means doing very little direct educating but co-ordinating a lot of others while trying to juggle diverse demands and keep a strategic perspective. In addition to those who work in the Education Department, there are 100 trained volunteers [p. 90] as well as the curators, freelance lecturers, artists, craftspeople, actors, story-tellers and musicians who also contribute to our programmes. Like many senior managers, I spend a lot of time in meetings. Planning the Great Court, for instance, involved endless meetings to devise the optimum facilities in the Clore Education Centre. My job is also entrepreneurial, working with and between the different worlds of fundraising and PR, exhibition and gallery design, educational TV, teacher training, publishing and museum studies and training all over the world. However, I am particularly interested in Asia, and have been since a child, so I have especially enjoyed working with the great variety of Japanese, Indian and Chinese art in the Museum.

Being one of many 'audience advocates' in the Museum means I try to interpret the needs of, say, art teachers or the Chinese community, or tour guides and tourists, and represent them in the planning of galleries and exhibitions, publications, programmes and policies. In return, educators are interpreting to various publics not just the collections and their cultural context but also the Museum itself, which is its own largest exhibit. Understanding the culture of museums is an important part of cultural understanding as a whole. The MA course I run jointly with the V&A and London University's Institute of Education looks at museums and galleries in education. I am also an external examiner for Britain's leading museum studies course in Leicester and I teach for other universities including an occasional video-conference link to Florida. So, in at least one area of my work, I do get immediate feedback – and it isn't another meeting!'

An Indian dance workshop in the Hotung Gallery.

The Museum responds whenever it can to educational demand and also tries to persuade its audiences to try out new approaches ('Not What You Expect', to quote a recent Science Week programme). The science education programme sponsored by Glaxo Wellcome brings the work of the two curatorial departments without galleries (Scientific Research and Conservation) to the attention of the public, giving scientists and conservators the opportunity to talk about and demonstrate their work in researching and preserving the collections, and responds, for example, to recent Government initiatives on numeracy and technology.

Linda Amrane-Cooper
Education

'A PhD in quantum mechanics may seem like a peculiar start to a career in museum education, but it has been really useful to have experience as a

A school group talks to a Museum scientist during National Science Week.

research scientist in doing this job. After a few years in research I decided that the isolation of theoretical physics was too great and I trained to be a teacher. As soon as I started in the classroom, I realized that I loved communicating about science. When, some years later, an opportunity came up for me to teach at the Ontario Science Centre in Canada, I leapt at it and found myself caught up in the exciting world of education within museums.

Working as the Science Education Officer has given me the wonderful opportunity to work with curators, scientists and conservators, helping to develop ways of presenting their work and the interwoven strands of science and technology throughout the Museum.

Most people do not expect to encounter science during a visit to The British Museum, yet science and technology are integral to its work and our events aim to illuminate this. For example, by showing visitors how to tell the time using the stars, we bring to life the astrolabe [see p. 48], a beautiful and important scientific instrument used by astronomers for hundreds of years in the medieval European and Islamic worlds. We demonstrate that science and technology are key in investigation of the objects by inviting visitors to peer down microscopes at Roman metalwork, explore cat mummies with the aid of CAT scans or discover the age of a bone by interrogating the radioactive carbon stored within it.'

An events programme, consisting of all the public events organized by Education, Marketing and Public Affairs and the curatorial departments, is published every two months. An unusual regular listing is the presentation of the Way of Tea. On the second and fourth Fridays of nearly every month, there are public demonstrations of the Japanese tea ceremony in the tea room in the Japanese galleries given by a leading member of the Urasenke school of tea. The Urasenke Foundation was one of the major donors who supported the building of the new Japanese galleries, which opened in 1990, and the tea room formed part of their contribution.

For many years until his untimely death in 1997, the ceremonies were

Tea ceremony in the Japanese tea room in the gallery.

performed by Michael Birch, a graduate of the Urasenke School in Kyoto. The present teacher is Sokei Kimura, who is assisted by his wife.

Sokei Kimura
Urasenke School

'Since arriving in London in 1997, our regular presentations of the Way of Tea at The British Museum have been an important part of our work in introducing this tradition to other cultures. The tea room was built in Japan with traditional Japanese materials and techniques and assembled by our own craftsmen in the gallery. The tea room has all the traditional elements, such as earthen walls, *tatami* mats covering the floor, a small crawling door, alcove and windows covered with paper.

We try our best to make the presentations as authentic as possible, giving visitors an idea of the atmosphere created in a Japanese traditional tea gathering. The *chashitsu* setting includes a calligraphic scroll and seasonal flowers; host and guests wear traditional kimono and usually someone from the public is invited to be part of the gathering in which sweets and *matcha* tea are served. We do have the most interesting reactions from the public when they are asked to take their shoes off, crawl into the room through the small door (70 x 70 cm), sit on the mats and drink the very bright green whisked beverage. The number of questions and interest from the audience is enormous after each presentation and to our delight some have become students of the Way of Tea.

We hope that our presentations and special events, such as a tea ceremony conducted in the presence of HRH the Duke of Gloucester by Urasenke School Master Nagai in May 1998, and an afternoon with the Young Friends of The British Museum, may bring a further understanding of Japanese culture and contribute to the Museum's educational programme.'

The Japanese Antiquities Department collects ambitiously (p. 68). Its small team of curators has mounted an astonishing range of exhibitions, particularly since its new galleries opened in 1990 in what was described as 'possibly the largest loft conversion in Europe'. Among other events, a Japanese master sword-polisher has demonstrated his craft, and a Japanese musician-composer has performed a dramatic percussion piece inspired by modern painted screens on show in the gallery. Numerous art students, ranging from seven- to seventy-year-olds, have been inspired by the sculpture, woodblock prints, paintings and armour. At one end of the Japanese galleries is the entrance to the Students' Room. Each antiquities department has a Students' Room, and they are an important part of the Museum's public service. The Prints and Drawings Students' Room is on the floor below the Japanese galleries.

Questions and answers

Jenny Ramkalawon
Prints and Drawings

'The Students' Room is the front line of the department, where we encounter everyone from A-level students to the heads of major institutions. Averaging 600 visitors per month, we are one of the busiest Students' Rooms in the Museum. The Print Room itself is a slightly imposing and intimidating room to the first-time visitor and so we try to be as friendly and informal as possible. One former colleague likened the job to waitressing. Over the past 10 years I have 'served up', amongst others, Michelangelo, Dürer and William Blake!

Some visitors come to the Print Room knowing exactly what they want to see. These tend to be university professors, other curators or dealers and they have the correct catalogue numbers and can be served with the minimum of fuss. We hope they leave satisfied that their researches have been conclusive. But I like best serving members of the public, some of whom have no art history background. Some are retired, some are merely pursuing a hobby. Often they are completely overwhelmed by what they have seen. They are truly grateful to have been allowed to look at a work of art close up with no barriers, no prohibitive messages. We bring them a box of prints or drawings, place them on an easel and leave them to it.

One American couple who came in quite by chance on their way to the airport requested to see some Leonardo drawings. They kept asking me if they were looking at 'the real thing' and were delighted when I assured them that they were. They could not believe that they had been allowed to come so close to a work of art. Many visitors come back year after year and are greeted like old friends by members of staff. My favourite students are those who come in having no idea what they want to see and leave feeling that they have encountered something more than the usual museum experience.'

Curators in The British Museum, like their colleagues elsewhere, spend a lot of time looking at objects that are not part of their own institution's collections. Most of these belong to members of the public who have found, inherited, bought or been given something odd or interesting which they want to know more about. The British Museum is the first port of call for many people, and many more are referred on from other museums, or indeed other institutions and individuals who have had good service in the past. All the Museum's curatorial departments have systems set up to deal with this and, as a result, most curators spend part of their working year performing this function.

Barrie Cook
Coins and Medals

'In Coins and Medals curators spend a week at a time on public enquiries, and each of us will take a turn every couple of months. You have to stay easily accessible during open hours and fit all other commitments and responsibilities around your duty. Also, it can get busy. Most years we identify 6,000 to 8,000 objects, and it is perfectly possible to get 50 or more a day. In the interests of fairness, we take only ten items a day from any one source, and, like all museums, what we cannot do is give valuations, to many visitors' disappointment. We simply are not qualified to do this.

Identifying a coin can take anything from a minute or two to several hours, and departmental colleagues might well have to be consulted. My own specialism is medieval coins, and while I have reasonable confidence in dealing with, say, medals, Roman and some Greek coins, this ebbs rapidly when faced with Islamic or Chinese material. Most of what one sees is straightforward enough for an experienced curator: if you don't know the answer immediately, you know where to look, or who to ask. And who could resist a feeling of smug satisfaction when recognizing something as Aksumite or from Cilician Armenia? Then, of course, you fail miserably with an easy-looking nineteenth-century token and have to confess defeat. You develop little rules and mantras: 'Always try Naples and Sicily' is one of mine. Every so often the miraculous happens, and you see something completely new. For me, the best such occasion was on seeing and identifying what is still the only example of the first-ever issue of English farthings, known from records of

Curator Irving Finkel giving an evening class on cuneiform in the Ancient Near Eastern Students' Room.

1220, but never known to exist until one turned up at the department in 1991. It made all the Victorian pennies and radiates of Tetricus worthwhile.'

Curators also give gallery talks and lectures, teach university students (often with objects from the reserve collections) and organize specialist seminars and conferences. When the first major exhibition on Burma in London since 1826 was arranged, the Museum collaborated with the School of Oriental and African Studies (University of London) to put on an international conference at which scholars working on Burmese art and archaeology could present their most recent research. This conference, which was funded by the Burma Project (New York), the Paul Hamlyn Foundation and the Charles Wallace (Burma) Trust, was a striking example of the Museum's role in championing new areas of research in world culture.

Richard Blurton
Oriental Antiquities

'The exhibition *Visions from the Golden Land* was prompted by the gift of the Isaacs collection of Burmese lacquer to the Museum in 1998. My own interest in Burma had developed following a visit in the early 1990s when I met Ruth and Ralph Isaacs, who were stationed in Rangoon on behalf of the British Council. Not only did I benefit from their famous hospitality, but I was also stimulated to think about two specific topics concerned with Burma. First, the way Burma has acted, just like Tibet, as a cultural reservoir, preserving many of the traditions of ancient India, specifically ancient Buddhist traditions that have long since disappeared in the subcontinent itself. And, secondly, the paucity of items within the Museum that demonstrated cultural activity in Burma since its independence in 1948. Ralph quickly showed me that both these topics could be addressed through one subject: the continuing production of lacquer in Burma. Fine work is still produced, can be purchased and could thus be added to the collections, and many items are still used in a Buddhist context, both monastic and secular.

As the culture of Burma is so little known, resources for an education programme were attached to the exhibition. The number of Burma scholars is both small and widely spread throughout the world, so it is rare for them to meet, discuss their new work and interact with others interested in Burma. None the less, I was amazed when our volunteer organizer, Alexandra Green, contacted potential speakers and found that 16 scholars wished to participate (I had anticipated six at the most). There was clearly a need for such a gathering, so we began to plan for a two-day meeting. Lecturers came from Australia, the US, Germany and France, as well as from the UK. Topics covered included prehistory, urbanism, inscriptions on lacquer vessels, manuscript and mural painting, sculpture, textiles and early photography.

In the end, between 50 and 60 people attended each of the four sessions, and the general consensus was that this was a significant event. Personally, it was rewarding to experience such a positive response and to have brought people together in a field that traditionally has few outlets. So encouraging was the response that we plan to publish the proceedings.'

Sometimes an events programme accompanies an exhibition when it travels abroad or in Britain. In 1997 the Museum organized with the British Council in India an extremely ambitious exhibition, *The Enduring Image*, as part of India's independence celebrations. This brought together sculpture, armour and jewellery on the theme of the human image in art and was seen in New Delhi and Bombay by over 150,000 people. Curators, conservators and educators collaborated with Indian colleagues on a conference, public lectures and events for teachers, children and families. Members of the Education Department have also, for example, run courses to accompany a loan exhibition on ancient Egypt in Singapore. They contribute to British Council programmes all over the world and welcome numerous foreign museum educators and curators in London.

The 24-hour museum

Events continue throughout the day at the Museum. School groups tend to leave by mid-afternoon, but art students are often still busy drawing in corners of basement galleries right up to closing time. The Museum's new longer opening hours, the Great Court and particularly the Clore Education Centre now make it possible to offer a much more ambitious evening programme. For many years The British Museum Friends (BMF) have organized monthly evening openings that are mainly for their members, but are also open to the public. The 13,000 Friends of The British Museum receive an excellent magazine and participate in a regular programme of lectures, tours and visits behind the scenes. Friends also contribute to the work of the Museum as volunteers, whether on the membership desks, as eyeOpener guides (p. 90), assisting at events or by helping with mailings.

Fiona Burtt
Public Events

'Since the end of 2000, visitors have been able to enjoy the wonders of the Museum until later in the evening on Thursdays and Fridays. But for many years, on the first Tuesday evening of every month except January, the Museum has closed as usual, then opened again at 6pm for three hours of special activities at our Evening Openings. Different galleries and exhibitions are open each month, and visitors can enjoy the Museum in a much more peaceful state than during the day, with a rich choice of gallery talks, lectures, live music and other activities, often focused on a particular theme.

In addition to managing a full programme of public events, and also special events for British Museum Friends, I have been organizing these evenings for the past two years, with the help of Events Assistant David Dinnage. Every year we have meetings with the curatorial departments to solicit ideas for themes and events and to discuss the most appropriate time of year to focus on specific areas of the collections. I then sketch out the programme for the year ahead, contact and book lecturers and work with designers to produce promotional leaflets for the evenings, while David books the speakers for gallery talks, arranges hands-on events, liaises with our music fixer and produces a programme. On the evening we have very little time to set up, so are generally seen only in a blur for half an hour before re-opening time. We are helped, however, by a host of BMF volunteers and staff. Once the initial entry rush has died down, the event generally ticks over calmly. I spend most of the evening introducing gallery talks, chatting to Friends and other visitors, making sure speakers are happy (and offering them a well-earned glass of wine after their talk), checking that all the events are going well and trouble-shooting as necessary.

By the end of the evening, we are usually exhausted after standing and smiling constantly for several hours! But there are three wonderful things about organizing these evenings: experiencing the magical atmosphere of the Museum after hours; having the opportunity to get to know colleagues from all over the Museum, from cleaners to curators; and, finally, feeling satisfied that hundreds of people have enjoyed themselves by the time we close the doors at 9pm.'

Evenings are also the time when teachers might come for a quiet, intensive look at new galleries or exhibitions as part of a 'twilight course', perhaps with a glass of wine in one hand and certainly without a school group to worry about. Outside organizations and companies may hire galleries in the evenings; the Museum hosts specialist lectures, including the first BP Lecture, which was given by Nelson Mandela. Or you can buy a ticket for a film, lecture or other special event. Between closing and re-opening to the public next morning the Museum doesn't sleep – a lot needs to be done before a new day begins.

Art students in one of the Wolfson basement galleries of Roman Sculpture.

Security staff work all through the night, while cleaners begin work at 7am in the galleries before moving on to offices and non-public areas. Queues form outside in Great Russell Street and coaches arrive at the north entrance in Montague Place long before the galleries and exhibitions open at 10am. The catering, bookshop and information desk staff in the Great Court also need to prepare for another busy day.

Help and advice

In 1997 the Department of Visitor Services was formed, encompassing the Information Service, the Museum's switchboard and, more recently, the gallery staff. With the opening of the Great Court, the Information Desk functions are expanding to incorporate other duties, not least the new Box Office. The primary purpose, however, remains the same: to assist visitors in enjoying their visit by providing detailed information on the Museum's collections, events and facilities.

Elizabeth Lewington
Visitor Services

'I started work in the Information Service in 1992 when the team was part of the Public Relations Office. I still remember vividly my first day on the Information Desk. After six weeks of trekking through 2½ miles of galleries to obtain 'the knowledge' and gaining a respectable mark from the 100-question test, I was set loose on the public. I thought all was going well until a colleague pointed out that an extremely bright red rash had spread over my neck and face and I realized that my voice had diminished to an unattractive croak. Luckily, my case of nerves lasted only a day and I soon discovered how much I enjoyed the diversity and unexpected nature of the role in such a demanding and front-line environment.

What do I look for when recruiting information assistants? The ability to remain calm and professional when a lost, screaming child has been deposited at the Information Desk is vital, as is a retentive memory; visitors really do want to know how many columns are outside the building and what classical order they conform to. Tact is indispensable, and was needed recently when a visitor demanded to see the British Museum's eminent archaeologist, Indiana Jones.

The information assistants are also expected to possess a thorough knowledge of other museums, galleries and tourist attractions, as well as bus routes, the nearest chemist and the best place for fish and chips on a Sunday evening! I am always keen to impress upon new staff that the greatest asset for an information assistant is not necessarily to know the answer, but to know where the answer can be found.'

Questions that have been asked at the Information Desk:

* What time is the 10.45am tour?

* Do you have a knitting pattern for a Viking jumper?

* Where are the Belgian Marbles?

* Have you got God's vest in the Museum?

* Do you hire out specimens? I want to borrow a giraffe.

* Is it true that you've got the oldest man in a jar here?

* Is your exhibition on ancient Egyptian gas masks still on?

* Do you have Jesus' manger here?

* I've read that you have Students' Rooms here – can I rent one for the summer?

* Is it true that Karl Marx worked at this Information Desk?

* How did they know it was BC?

* Where is the Risotto Stone?

* Where can I see the Hanging Basket of Babylon?

Early visitors can now sit and drink a cup of coffee in the Great Court, admiring a view of the building not seen since the mid nineteenth century, while staff begin to take up positions in more than 90 galleries. Formerly known as warders, they are now gallery staff and are part of Visitor Services, a department of the Marketing and Public Affairs Directorate. When the Museum first opened in the eighteenth century, the galleries were 'protected from the public' by soldiers, stationed north of the Museum. The Metropolitan Police then took over, followed by retired police officers. The term gallery warder came into being in 1934. With improvements in security technology, the role of the gallery warder is being developed to provide greater assistance for the diverse needs of the many visitors to The British Museum. There are over 150 gallery staff and they play an essential role within the Museum. Many have first-aid knowledge, foreign language skills and, if not, usually find an innovative way to impart relevant information. Gallery assistants are also essential when emergency circumstances require the Museum to be evacuated.

Lorna Lee
Visitor Services

'I joined the Department of Conservation in 1985 as a conservation scientist and spent 12 enjoyable years researching a myriad of materials, from pigments on Egyptian coffins to corrosion on medieval lead. However, I wanted to get more involved with the public face of the Museum, and when Visitor Services was formed I applied for the new post of Visitor Services Manager. I now spend my time developing ways to improve all services for the visitors, which involves a great deal of liaison with almost every department in the Museum, and maintaining strong links with other institutions in London and beyond.

To ensure that the Museum, its facilities and services meet expectations, Visitor Services has expanded and now incorporates gallery staff. Each member acts as the eyes and the ears of the Museum, and their feedback provides extremely useful information when trying to assess whether visitors have enjoyed their visit or where they have encountered difficulties. The cloak room provides an essential service to visitors, and everyday items such as hats and coats are normally deposited. The occasional unexpected item turns up at lost property – it was a rather red-faced visitor who turned up to claim their full set of false teeth. Despite a sometimes challenging and tiring role, gallery staff often find their day lightened by humorous moments. One afternoon a gallery supervisor overheard a couple viewing the Magna Carta, before its transfer to the new British Library. The husband asked the supervisor 'When was this signed?' The supervisor replied '1215', at which the wife berated her husband: 'If you had got up earlier we could have *seen* it being done!''

The Great Court project

The development of the Great Court – the British Museum's equivalent of the spectacular glass pyramid in the courtyard of the Louvre, or the many new wings to be found in North American art museums – has at last made it possible for the Museum to provide properly for the needs of its many publics. The transformation of the space only recently vacated by the British Library has been dramatic, the result of work by many staff in the Museum, as well as outside architects and contractors. The new circulation space will relieve some of the pressure on galleries, where visitors will be able to take their time in viewing the displays. The Great Court project also includes the development of the Reading Room, which will allow access to first-class facilities such as the COMPASS database and The Paul Hamlyn Library in the Walter and Leonore Annenberg Centre.

Chris Jones
Operations

'It is a project sponsor's lot to try to satisfy all of the people all of the time, despite the fact that it is in the nature of projects, as in life, that this ideal is rarely if ever achieved. There is always something new, always a surprise around the corner. Often frustrating, but always fascinating and almost addictive. Immersion in this project has opened my eyes wider to the fascination of architecture, and now everywhere I go I find myself gazing at buildings to see how they work.

All projects need precise and complete definition. So a clear brief, with no gaps and no room for misunderstanding, is a must. How did we do with the Great Court? Well, not badly, and such changes as we did make I excuse on the basis that they were either necessary to maintain budget and programme or, despite the challenge presented by making them, they have improved the quality of the project. One amazing fact often overlooked about the Great Court project is that, although it has been undertaken in the very heart of our site, we have not closed the Museum for a single day during construction. Many museums and galleries around the world have closed their doors at such times, and for much smaller projects. The construction of the Great Court has been compared to converting the loft in your home and taking all materials, out or in, through the letter-box!

I will not attempt to describe the project in detail; it needs to be seen and experienced. Suffice to say that it is the most important piece of building work undertaken at the Museum for a century. It changes the face of the Museum entirely and allows the visitor to access the building from its heart instead of having to trudge around the perimeter. It houses new galleries, a new Education Centre, shops, a café, a restaurant and essential services such as lifts, toilets and first aid. And the fabulous Round Reading Room is restored to its former glory and available to all for the first time. Come and see it.'

Recording the Great Court project as it developed has involved archaeologists (p. 61), archivists (p. 62), a video team and photographers.

Dudley Hubbard
Photography and Imaging

'Often I do not know what sort of work I will be doing from day to day and when the phone rings I know that very soon I'll be away on another *sortie*. This wasn't the case with the Great Court, however. Simon Tutty and I were asked to provide progress shots for the various building companies and for the Museum. We attended safety courses and were kitted out with helmets,

A simulated aerial view of the Great Court.

boots and high-visibility jackets. Two tower cranes were erected over the Museum and I realized that we had to have access to these in order to get some aerial views. We had to push to get permission, though once we had been up and shown off our images the requests started pouring in. After each visit we're busy typing out labels to ensure that dates and facts are accurately recorded alongside each image. Shots taken at every opportunity have now given us a valuable historical record of what will undoubtedly be one of the biggest visitor attractions in London.

We have had to record premises prior to demolition (due to our status as a listed building with an obligation to English Heritage) and this has taken us from the underfloor area of the Reading Room to a 'Manrider' cage dangling from the crane over the top of the same building.'

In the centre of the Great Court, now restored to its original splendour, is the famous Round Reading Room in which Karl Marx wrote *Das Kapital*. A special display shows how many other authors have worked there since it opened in 1857. This famous building has now found a new role as a freely accessible public information centre, generously funded by Walter and Leonore Annenberg. Fifty terminals give access to COMPASS (p. 109) and the ground floor of bookcases now houses a completely new library, funded by publisher and philanthropist Paul Hamlyn.

Pam Smith
Education

'I studied classics at university and while a student took part in some of the early excavations at Fishbourne Palace, so building the collection for The Paul Hamlyn Library enabled me to combine a special personal interest with my professional experience. To set up a new library is a rare and exciting challenge. It is also a great responsibility, particularly when the library is housed in the world-famous Reading Room at The British Museum. It was my task to select, order, catalogue and process the initial stock for this new public reference library, which opened in December 2000.

The subject coverage of the new library is as extensive as the collections of the Museum itself, and we anticipated a wide range of users – children, students, visitors to the Museum and interested members of the public. I spent many happy hours browsing in bookshops and libraries and scanning publishers' catalogues for relevant titles. In addition to deciding which books to buy, I advised on their arrangement, as we wanted the library to be as accessible as possible. After all, this is the first time in its history that the Reading Room will be freely open to the public.

A small team of library staff was kept very busy ordering, cataloguing and, with the help of many enthusiastic volunteers, processing the books ready for the shelves in the Reading Room. Temporary storage space was provided in the magnificent bookpresses in the King's Library (some Museum visitors thought the British Library was moving back!). It has been wonderful to watch the collection grow and I feel very fortunate to have been involved in this unique project.'

Kate Channing
British Museum Company

Wrapped around the outside of the Reading Room are visitor facilities including shops run by The British Museum Company. Over three years the retail team closed four shops to make way for Great Court building work, relocated to two temporary shops and performed eight shop openings, while continuing to run a shop at Heathrow Terminal 4 and three gallery shops focusing on the Museum's changing exhibition programme.

'My role as the Head of Retail has been to develop the vision of how our shops should look once the Great Court was open and how we should provide customer service to meet the needs of our many visitors. The job is an ideal blend of the creative, the practical and the commercial. It took six months of researching the way the shops ran, what they sold and what the staff and customers wanted to see happening in them before I was able to write the shop design brief. We set up a project team including retail design specialists, who worked closely with the architects and construction team to understand the unique qualities of the Great Court.

The shop designs were developed as a result of many hours of discussion in which we analysed our products, their packaging, how they represent the Museum, how we price them, where we store them, how we light them, what hours we are open, what our shops look like when they are closed, and hundreds of other issues. Personally, I particularly enjoy finding unusual products for our shops and analysing our sales information to determine what new products we should commission to keep our shops fresh and interesting.'

Multimedia

Like all major museums, The British Museum now also reaches a worldwide audience through the Internet. Over five million people visit the Museum each year, but five or six times that number visit it virtually or use one of its websites. COMPASS, which stands for COllections Multimedia Public AccesS System, is a computer system that provides information about a selection of items in The British Museum. Aimed at general visitors, it includes text descriptions and background information, and provides very high-quality images and 3D reconstruction. A modified version of what is available via the 50 special terminals in the restored Reading Room is also available on the Internet. This has been designed to be accessible to those without the latest PC technology and users with visual impairments. In 2001 an educational version, aimed initially at children aged 8–11 and their teachers, is being launched.

The team is made up of specialists in a number of areas, who process material provided by writers and photographers so that it is suitable for COMPASS. It took two and a half years to develop the COMPASS system and during that time over 90 of the Museum's curators wrote material about the objects and the COMPASS team edited over 1,000,000 words of

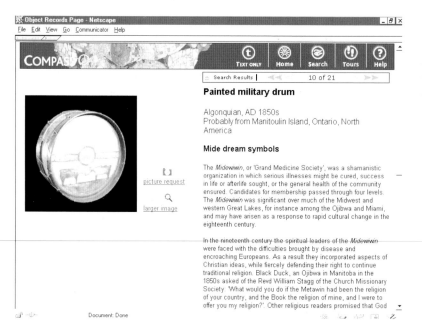

COMPASS, which has been funded by a generous donation from the Annenberg Foundation, can be found on the web at: http://www.thebritishmuseum.ac.uk/compass.

text and processed over 5,000 images. Three editors worked on text received from curators, providing a consistent style, adding hyperlinks between items and indexing each in the database. Three imaging specialists used computers to prepare images of the objects. Computer reconstructions of people, places and artefacts were created by the COMPASS 3D design team, who worked with curators to ensure that the virtual world re-creates what the Museum has developed through its research and expertise. Schools are an important audience with specific needs, and the team also includes an education specialist, who works with the Education Department to produce curriculum resources for teachers and pupils. Completing the COMPASS team are a support officer, content manager and project manager, who deal with finance, intellectual property and commissioning freelance writers.

David Jillings
COMPASS

'After he won his fourth Olympic gold medal Steve Redgrave said, 'If you ever see me in a boat again, shoot me'. Yet in 2000 he won his fifth. I said something similar about national museums when I left the V&A seven years ago, yet here I am again. In more than twenty years in the civil service I have had a range of jobs, including paying benefits to the homeless over the counter in the DHSS, sitting as clerk of court in the Lands Tribunal, and working on national IT projects in the Court Service and DoE. I might not have come back to museums if it had not been for COMPASS, but it was a chance too good to miss. This is by far the most exciting project, as well as the most challenging, I have ever come across.

There is more to COMPASS than any system I have worked on before. Creating the content, text, images and effects has been like writing a book. The content needs a means of delivery, and in this case there are two: the

COMPASS website and the terminals in the new Annenberg Centre. All ICT systems need an interface, but very few people design their own computer terminal from scratch. To meet our requirements for the highest quality screens within the constraints of the Annenberg Centre, we have had to become engineers of hardware as well as information systems.

When I arrived at The British Museum at Christmas in 1997, my first tasks were to recruit a full-time project team, find a set of offices and identify a supplier with the skills and experience to build the system. For the first few months I was hidden away on my own in various spare corners, with plenty of time for thinking and planning, and few phone calls, meetings or e-mails. Now I share an office with a busy team and have all too many distractions. In between I try to work out how to manage my job to get the best of both these worlds. It has been a privilege to be part of The British Museum and of COMPASS, and I am not ready to be shot just yet.'

Fiona Marshall
COMPASS

'For me it all started with a gas radio ... Twenty years ago I was an information scientist running one of the British Gas libraries – which included a Gas Museum. Hooked on working with unique objects, I moved to Leicestershire Museums, co-ordinating the recording of information about collections. After twelve years managing a great variety of information and computer projects, many involving collaboration with a number of national museums, I was lucky enough to be offered this job.

As COMPASS Content Manager I co-ordinate the work of a dedicated team of multimedia specialists, curators and other staff all around the Museum who are putting together information for COMPASS. Behind the COMPASS system is a sophisticated database. The database allows us to index the objects and keep track of content writing, editing and checking.

One of the most enjoyable aspects of the job, apart from walking through our historic galleries full of wonderful objects every morning, is the chance to work with curators who are world experts in their fields. The team effectively acts as an intermediary between the curators and the users of COMPASS.

It is vital, of course, that we provide our visitors with something they want and can use, so we have talked to different groups and tried to make the system as accessible as possible. The COMPASS team is converting the curators' knowledge and enthusiasm for their subjects into a high-quality, educational and, we hope, enjoyable presentation.'

Schools, teachers and adult learners have particular needs in accessing Museum collections, expertise and information. ICT provision for them has been pioneered in the Education Department. IT is the means: the C stands for communication, the crucial ingredient for all these projects.

Rowena Loverance
Education

'Now that the new technology is all around us, it takes quite an effort of imagination to remember those heady days when its educational potential first began to dawn. At that time I was a museum education officer, giving

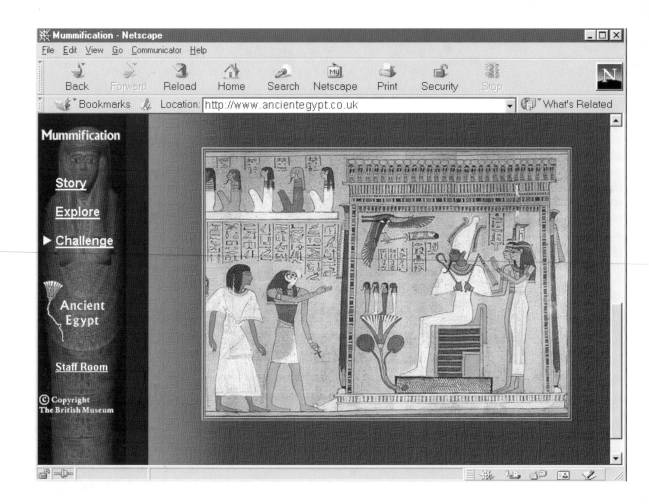

A page from the Ancient Egypt website at: http://www.ancientegypt.co.uk.

the usual lectures and gallery talks and producing paper and video resources. I was lucky enough to have the opportunity to develop an early CD-Rom, which became *The Anglo-Saxons Interactive*, and I saw for myself the huge educational excitement in using multimedia to link and make available different kinds of resources. With these means it was possible to tell stories to audiences in different ways at the same time, and to present more material in higher quality than had ever been possible. Since those early days, the rapid development of the Internet has added the ability to communicate instantaneously with museum audiences.

Ten years on, I've raised the money and hired an in-house team to create and deliver educational multimedia. Our first product, launched in autumn 1999, was *Ancient Egypt* [www.ancientegypt.co.uk], the first of a series of web-based modules for schools called 'Ancient Civilizations'. All the old favourites of the British Museum's collections are there – mummies, 'Ginger', the Rosetta Stone – but you can also search for gold up the Nile, measure the Great Pyramid in terms of double-decker buses, and dare the hazards of the Egyptian underworld protected only by three spells. The website experiments with presenting content in different ways: in linear story form, as a self-guided exploration and with online activities or challenges. In this way I hope that as well as encouraging people to learn about ancient Egypt in a more exciting way, we shall also be evaluating how people learn using new technology.

Among appreciative comments from the site's users, Class 5NL at Greneway School, Royston, wrote: 'We have just visited your Ancient Egypt site. It was very interesting and exciting and well-organized. We liked the challenges, they were excellent. The pyramid story was cool.' A hospital school in Mannheim, Germany, wrote: 'I have never found better materials in other well-known museums on the Internet. We are very much looking forward to your future website about Mesopotamia.'

As well as Mesopotamia, future plans include learning resources for adults on Islamic art, in partnership with sites and museums from countries in the Arab and Islamic world. We have also begun trialling new kinds of online learning for both children and adult groups in our new on-site facilities in the Museum's Clore Education Centre in the Great Court.'

Teaching and learning

The Education Department also provides many other kinds of help and encouragement for teachers, during their initial training as well as later on, and for children and families.

Richard Woff
Education

'The whole of my working life has been connected in some way with schools. First I taught in London comprehensives, then became a teacher educator in the University of London and now, as Deputy Head of Education, my principal responsibility is the Museum's provision for children, young people in general, schools and teachers. Although school students represent a small proportion of the visitors to the Museum, they are critically important – if children are put off on their first visit to the Museum, they are less likely to come back as adults. And since schools bring all their children, rich or poor, museum-motivated or not, they are one of the few ways that the Museum can be assured of reaching the full range of people living in Britain.

I spend most of my time co-ordinating and helping colleagues who are preparing resources, activity materials, teaching sessions and other programmes to make that first visit as stimulating as possible. We always try to suggest to teachers ways that they can prepare their children for a visit, what they can do when they are here, and how they can use the experience later back at school.

It is important to keep up with the relentless flow of initiatives in the world of education, from changes to the national curriculum to the promotion of out-of-school learning. This involves lots of reading and regular liaison with bodies such as the Qualifications and Curriculum Authority and the Department for Education and Employment. I also develop collaboration with schools TV, educational magazines and a wide range of special projects so as

Taking part in a Roman Army Day with the Ermine Street Guard.

to reach as many schools as possible and maximize the impact of the Museum's contribution.

I love working directly with teachers and children, but I have to ration myself strictly. I do most of my teaching with student teachers – it seems to me doubly dynamic, in that reaching one teacher means reaching at least 30 children annually, and in getting at the teachers early in their careers, I can multiply the effect over 40 years!'

The Education Department produces resource packs to help teachers, students and adult learners to use new galleries, such as those for North America or Africa, and educational websites are in production for the Ancient Near East, China and India, cultures largely ignored in the national school curriculum. Increasingly, the emphasis is on participation and hands-on programmes, inviting children to meet Pythagoras, live in Benin, excavate in Egypt or go shopping in an Aztec market. A highly successful recent development has been the Arab World programme sponsored by the Karim Rida Said Foundation. This builds on the many popular Arab World exhibition programmes at the Museum of Mankind created by former curator Shelagh Weir. These included *Nomad and City*, with its memorable evocation of an Arab souk, and *Palestinian Costume* with its resident Palestinian museum educator, Sonia el-Nimr (who is now in charge of museums in Palestine).

Carolyn Perry
Education

'I wanted to work at The British Museum when I was very young, so I still get a thrill in the morning when I collect my bunch of keys! I've worked in universities and schools, and was an eyeOpener guide [p. 90] in the Islamic Gallery before I joined the Education Department. I now run the Arab World

Education Programme, which means that I use the Museum's collections to help people learn more about Arab culture and history. My job is never the same two days in a row as it involves working with lots of different audiences, collections and curators around the Museum. It is also split between programme planning and actually delivering events and activities. One day I could be giving a lecture on the influence of Islam on art in nineteenth-century Britain,

Tunisian craftsman at work during an Arab World event.

and the next day you will find me serving Arabic tea and coffee in a Bedouin tent, helping people to learn about the Arab world in an informal way. I have organized study days on Yemen, Tunisia, Cairo, Lebanon and Saudi Arabia, attracting a mixture of academic and interested adult audiences.

One of the most important parts of my work is to try to counteract stereotyping about Arabs and their culture. I ran a project linked to the *Writing Arabic* exhibition [p. 33] which travelled to several parts of the UK, asking young people to respond to objects from different Arab countries. They made up stories, wrote labels for their chosen objects and also produced their own works of art, which were later exhibited at the Museum.

When we asked each person what they thought of when they heard the word 'Arab', young people with Arab backgrounds told us about large welcoming families, wide open spaces and houses with flat roofs where they could play. This was in contrast to the non-Arab young people who listed camels, sand and men with baggy trousers and curved swords. It seems that for many young people in Britain today, Aladdin is the most famous Arab in the world! We hope, through activities and events, to give everyone a greater understanding (and a less stereotypical view) of a fascinating culture.'

One of the young participants in the *Writing Arabic* project commented:

Hafsah Saeid
Exeter

'If there was another project I would recommend it to anyone who has an Arab background because it's fun. You get to be around people who are like you so you don't feel quite as embarrassed to talk about things you normally wouldn't around people who are Christian, say, and who don't know what it feels like for people who have a different background from the main culture in Britain.'

Outreach is at the heart of the access programme, which builds on pioneering work at the Museum by Anne Pearson and later Sue Picton in developing handling collections, touch exhibitions, galleries with touch tours and other facilities for our diverse and numerous visitors with disabilities. The introduction of the Disability Discrimination Act now requires museums to address their needs, although many have been seeking to do so for some time.

Kate Ramsden
Education

'Should you deny someone access to a museum's collections, programmes or events because they are disabled? As Access Officer, it is my job to ensure that the answer to that question is 'No'. This is done by developing and encouraging the participation of disabled people in all areas of museum life.

Two years ago I moved to The British Museum from Leeds, where I had been working as a learning support lecturer for half the week. The other half was taken up with teaching adults who had returned to education. Working at the Museum has drawn on the skills I had and allowed me to develop others. I particularly enjoy working with people from a wide range of backgrounds and previous experience. My role encompasses everything from the creation of large-print labels for exhibitions, organizing the interpretation of gallery talks into British Sign Language, to supporting the role of the Disability Working Party. This forum encourages Museum departments to discuss access issues and work collaboratively towards solutions. I work closely with colleagues in the Education Department and with curators, as they are the subject experts. It is my job to ensure that information is delivered in an accessible way. We try to arrange events for as wide an audience as possible, and many of these are practical activities that are inspired by Museum objects.

A gallery talk on Chinese art is sign-interpreted.

One of the most rewarding and enjoyable elements of my job is developing links with groups who do not think the Museum would have anything to offer them. I was delighted when a group of students from the college where I worked in Leeds came to visit The British Museum during Adult Learners' Week. For many of them it was the first time they had been to London and a small group of them have already been back. The main challenge I now face is not any longer persuading staff to participate in projects and initiatives, but co-ordinating their ideas about the collections and how specific audiences might work with them. This change in attitude is not only a response to new legislation but also a gratifying result of our extensive programme of training in disability equality.'

Wonder and learning, enjoyment and excitement, access and inclusion are at the heart of what the Museum hopes to achieve. The many components of the Great Court are only a beginning; the future holds new challenges, new building sites and new audiences.

CHAPTER 6

Looking Ahead

The British Museum is going through a period of profound change. Like many other major Millennium projects, it now looks and feels different in terms of space, organization and appearance. The departure of the British Library produced 40 per cent more space, and the creation of the Great Court in part of that space has given the Museum lungs and a heart. In the past visitors were pushed around the edges of the building and what was worthy of interest was dictated by the hierarchy of spaces; now they can go first to the centre to determine what they want to see. They may opt to visit the galleries for Mexico, Japan or Celtic Europe, as well as Greece or Egypt. The Museum is a pleasanter environment, with more places to sit, eat and drink, and with several special exhibitions to choose from. The famous Round Reading Room is not a limited-access library for scholars any longer, but a superb library and information centre (p. 108) for anyone who wishes to pursue an interest sparked off by one of the galleries, most of which have been renewed in the last decade. Extended opening hours now relate to normal twenty-first-century lives. Audiences – both on-site and virtual – will probably grow considerably and will certainly be more critical and more diverse in their demands, spending more time in the Museum and more money in the shops and restaurant. More visitors will find it worthwhile to become Friends, to sign up for classes, to volunteer, to meet friends here in the evenings or bring their children at weekends.

The old West Central Post Office sorting office, at the opposite end of Museum Street, is destined to become the Museum's new Study Centre.

Museums are in competition for audiences and attention not only with each other, but also with other leisure attractions that may be less demanding and seem on the surface to be more fun. An age of almost global mass culture has not deserted museums, however; more people go to museums in Britain than to the theatre or to football matches, and there is much more media and educational interest than ever before. We should be reassured that there is a growing hunger for the real alongside and perhaps because of the omnipresence of the simulated and filtered experience in the virtual world of today. But what is a *British* Museum for, now and in the future? What narratives of Britishness past and present can this Museum offer to the multicultural Britain of the twenty-first century? There are national museums in Cardiff, Belfast and Edinburgh but no English museum, nor was The British Museum ever intended to be that. The idea of such international museums remains controversial in an age of persisting nationalisms. Because it attracts such a diverse international audience, the Museum has the potential to encourage greater international understanding. Visitors from all over the world see evidence of cultures, past and present, with which they may be more familiar (not necessarily their own), alongside the unfamiliar. Facilitating that connection is one of the many challenges we face, as globalization and prejudice remain yoked together.

A museum can only partially paraphrase the world: in one building in central London you are invited to sample several prehistories, many long-lasting urbanized cultures, a slice of Britain, a bit of the history of world sculpture, a flavour of Africa. Public access to objects that are not on display remains a major challenge, although Students' Rooms (p. 98) and temporary exhibitions already try to answer this need. From 2003 it is hoped that the Study Centre will do a great deal more. Only a block away from the Museum, it will become home for six of the thirteen curatorial departments, plus the Clothworkers' Centre for World Textiles (p. 71) and an array of new hands-on and study facilities for archaeology, textiles, ethnography, art and science. This will give a whole new meaning to 'access' to the Museum, its collections, activities and expertise.

As it approaches its 250th anniversary in 2003, The British Museum has a challenging agenda of renewal. In achieving this it will seek a new balance between the many demands on its resources – between on-site and off-site activity, whether exhibitions or fieldwork, between developing the real and the virtual visitor experience, between the permanent and the temporary, the displayed and the stored collections, the popular and the scholarly. However much appearances, presentation and communication may change, everything the Museum does is still underpinned by the expertise and energy of its staff, by their research and shared insights into the collections, their contribution to visitors' experiences and the smooth running of a large institution. Research into collections is increasingly combined with research into audiences, their expectations

Cultures meeting at a family event for Chinese New Year.

and their experience of the Museum. This will fuel not only many new and renewed galleries and exhibitions, new events and publications, but also new types of communication and connection, not least about contemporary arts and societies as well as what most of our visitors expect to see. As each generation fashions its own histories, so museums have to respond and participate in this wider debate.

The King's Library is the centrepiece of the 2003 celebrations – the restoration and interpretation of the oldest part of the Museum and also the installation of a new display that looks back to the confidence of the Age of Enlightenment, a confidence almost unimaginable now. The founding fathers of the 1750s could still expect to embrace in one institution all areas of knowledge and their interconnectedness. As it turned out, such a Smithsonian scale of ambition could not be contained under one roof and the Museum has gradually become more specialized and focused. However, with the increasingly flexible and internationally available use of new technologies, with new patterns of leisure and learning, it is perhaps possible 250 years later to anticipate a new bringing together of Museum and publics, of knowledge and experience, even though audiences are so much bigger, more varied and demanding than ever before, and knowledge and styles of learning so much more diverse.

A major museum is one of the few reliable, permanent but flexible resources for lifelong learning to which we can return as and when we feel the need throughout our lives. It can combine the advantages of a library with the inspiration and challenge of the real object and the unexpected experience, plus the support of every kind of interpretation from website, family event or school visit to scholarly conference or tourist tour. With the completion of the Study Centre, the Museum will become a campus for lifelong learning in two buildings. This will be the biggest step yet in taking you, the curious museum visitor, behind the scenes at The British Museum.

FURTHER INFORMATION

The most accessible source of further information about The British Museum is its own website (http://www.thebritishmuseum.ac.uk).

The Museum is governed by an Act of Parliament, the British Museum Act 1963. The Act does not give any detailed guidance, but lays down that the Museum should have 25 Trustees, mostly appointed by the Prime Minister but also some by the Queen and various learned bodies such as the British Academy. The Act imposes a duty on the Trustees to keep the collection in the Museum, unless some objects are being sent on loan, and to make it available to members of the public. It forbids the disposal of anything in the collection, with certain limited exceptions.

The Museum is financed from both public and private sources. At the moment it costs about £45m to run every year. It receives about two-thirds of this as an allocation from the Department for Culture, Media and Sport, the government department with overall responsibility for the Museum. The other third is made up of direct income on sales (e.g. books, photographs, hiring out parts of the Museum for corporate entertainment) and sponsorship. Major donations are essential for the capital development of the Museum, since it is so expensive. Most new gallery projects have a private sponsor, and big projects like the Great Court and Study Centre need a mixture of external funding. The Great Court, with a budget of £97.9m, is funded with about £46m of money from the Millennium and Heritage Lottery Funds, but the remaining sum, over £50m, has been raised from private sources.

The Trustees appoint the Museum's senior management. At the time of writing the Museum has two directors who report directly to the Trustees: a director who is responsible for the curatorial and academic side of the Museum, and a managing director who is responsible for its good running and finances.

The senior executive body in the Museum is the Museum Management Board, which is supported by the Planning Committee and the Keepers' Committee. Other business is transacted by other internal committees, all of which report to one or other of these three.

The two directors are responsible for the Museum's main departments. The collection, scientific and public departments are together responsible for the collection and for most of the Museum's direct dealings with the public, and they are backed up by several administrative and infrastructure departments, as well as other affiliated bodies.

Collection departments

The Department of the Ancient Near East covers the ancient civilizations of the Near East from the Neolithic period until the coming of Islam in the seventh century AD, and its holdings amount to some 280,000 objects. Areas include Iraq, Iran, Central Asia, Syria, ancient Palestine, Phoenician settlements in the western Mediterranean, Anatolia, Transcaucasia and the Arabian Peninsula. The holdings of Assyrian, Babylonian and Sumerian antiquities are among the most comprehensive in the world.

The Department of Egyptian Antiquities houses one of the most important collections of its kind outside Cairo. The collection of about 110,000 objects illustrates every aspect of ancient Egyptian culture from Predynastic times (c. 4000 BC) down to the Coptic (Christian) period (twelfth century AD), and includes a significant amount of material from Nubia and the Sudan.

The Department of Greek and Roman Antiquities covers the Greek world from the beginning of the Bronze Age (about 3500 BC), Italy from the Bronze Age (about 2200 BC) and the Roman world up until the fourth century AD. It is one of the most comprehensive collections of antiquities from the civilizations of Greece and Rome with over 100,000 objects. The Greek collections include the Cycladic, Minoan and Mycenaean cultures.

The Department of Prehistory and Early Europe holds some 3,000,000 objects dating from the Old Stone Age, Neolithic, Bronze and Iron Ages, and artefacts from Roman Britain. The Old Stone Age collections come from all over Africa, South Asia and Western Europe with some more recent artefacts made by prehistoric hunter-gatherers in the Americas and Australasia, and include a major collection of European works of art and jewellery made on bone, antler and ivory, contemporaneous with cave paintings dating from 35,000 to 10,000 years ago. The Neolithic, Bronze Age and Iron Age collections contain antiquities from all over Europe but best represent the prehistory of Britain. The Roman collections reflect all aspects of life in the province of Britannia from the first to the early fifth century AD.

The Department of Medieval and Modern Europe covers European art and archaeology from the fourth to the twentieth centuries. The outstanding collections of some 230,000 objects illustrate many aspects of European cultures and some non-European Christian and Jewish cultures from the early Middle Ages to the twentieth century. The department houses the national collections of Anglo-Saxon antiquities, sealdies, medieval pottery, icons and horology.

The Department of Oriental Antiquities covers the cultures of Asia from the Neolithic period to the present day. The collection of some 140,000 objects includes paintings and prints from all areas as well as antiquities and sculpture in all media. The collections of sculpture from the Indian subcontinent are the most comprehensive in Europe. The

Museum holds outstanding collections of Chinese antiquities, paintings and porcelain and a broad range of Islamic pottery, tiles, metalwork, glass, seals and inscriptions.

The Department of Japanese Antiquities holds one of the most comprehensive collections of Japanese material culture in Europe, comprising about 25,000 objects. The collection includes early archaeological material; the arts of Buddhism; secular paintings, prints and printed books; secular sculpture; metalwork, including swords and sword furniture; textiles; lacquerware; and ceramics, including porcelain and tea ceremony wares and utensils.

The Department of Ethnography's collections comprise some 300,000 objects, representing the cultures of indigenous peoples throughout the world. Their scope is both contemporary and historical, focusing on Africa, Asia and the Middle East, Oceania, the Americas and Eastern Europe. The bulk of the material was acquired in the nineteenth and twentieth centuries and largely dates from this time.

The Department of Coins and Medals has one of the world's finest collections, containing some 650,000 objects. The magnificent coin collection covers the history of coinage from its origins in the seventh century BC to the present day, and includes related material such as coin weights, tokens and toy money. The department also holds the national collection of paper money, containing notes ranging from fourteenth-century China to current issues from banks all over the world.

The Department of Prints and Drawings holds one of the most representative and distinguished collections of Western prints and drawings. The collection contains approximately 3,000,000 works on paper from the fifteenth century to the present day, covering the entire history of the major graphic arts as well as including important collections of ephemera. The greatest strengths of the collection lie in the fields of Old Master prints and drawings from all schools, satires of the eighteenth and nineteenth centuries, and British material of all periods. Since the mid-1970s particular attention has been given to improving the representation of work executed from the late nineteenth century to the present day.

Scientific departments

The Department of Conservation is one of the largest museum conservation facilities in the world. Its main role is to clean, repair and restore the objects in the Museum collections and also to ensure that they have the best possible environmental conditions. Conservation scientists are involved in research into why objects deteriorate, methods of arresting deterioration, methods for cleaning, repairing and restoring, and the properties of new materials for use in conservation.

The Department of Scientific Research undertakes research on the

Museum's collections, focusing on the composition, technology of manufacture, provenance and date of objects. It also provides scientific and computer services including programs for the documentation of the Museum's collections (pp. 83–4) and their display on the Museum website via the COMPASS project (pp. 109–11).

Public departments

The Education Department promotes learning at all levels. It aims to make the Museum more accessible for its varied audiences by providing advice, teaching and materials to specific target groups: children, whether in family or school groups; students and teachers from schools, colleges and universities; and adults.

The Directorate of Marketing and Public Affairs is responsible for the presentation of the Museum to all its publics, managing visitor services, design, photography, exhibitions, the website, market research, corporate services, membership development, promotion and public relations.

Administrative and infrastructure departments

The Department of Operations is responsible for all matters relating to buildings and accommodation, maintenance, computers and telecommunications, security and fire safety, health and safety, both at the Bloomsbury site and at outstations.

The Department of Human Resources is responsible for all staffing policies, including recruitment, promotion, pay, appraisal, conduct and discipline, and training.

The Department of Finance is responsible for setting the Museum's budgets for earned income, current expenditure, capital projects and purchases for the collections; for operating the management accounting system, and monitoring and controlling income and expenditure; for administration of trust funds; for payments and receipts; for making contracts; and for producing the annual accounts.

Affiliated bodies

The British Museum Company, a limited company owned by the Trustees, has three divisions. These are responsible for retailing in Bloomsbury and elsewhere; publishing 55–60 books each year and producing merchandise including replicas, jewellery and gifts; and operating tours to places of cultural interest. In 1997–8 its turnover was £9.3m, and it gave profits of £1.75m to the Museum.

The British Museum Development Trust is responsible for fundraising for a broad range of Museum projects. The main recent project has been the Great Court, and the next phase includes the Study Centre and the King's Library.

The British Museum Friends is a membership organization which exists to support the Museum. Its 13,000 members benefit from exhibition entry and previews, a regular magazine and a substantial programme of behind-the-scenes activities. Every year it donates between £100,000 and £150,000 to the Museum for acquisitions.

The American Friends of The British Museum initiates fundraising in the USA and organizes cultural events there.

Further reading

E. Miller, *That Noble Cabinet: A History of the British Museum* (British Museum Publications, 1973)

D.M. Wilson, *The British Museum: Purpose and Politics* (British Museum Publications, 1989)

M. Caygill, *The Story of the British Museum* (2nd edn, British Museum Press, 1992)

E. Hooper-Greenhill, *Museums and the shaping of knowledge* (Routledge, 1992)

T. Bennett, *The Birth of the Museum* (Routledge, 1995)

C. Duncan, *Civilising Rituals: Inside public art museums* (Routledge, 1995)

M. Caygill, *A–Z Companion to the British Museum* (British Museum Press, 1999)

R. Anderson, *The Great Court and The British Museum* (British Museum Press, 2000)

M. Caygill, *An Illustrated History of the Reading Room* (British Museum Press, 2000)

A new history of The British Museum is being written by D.M. Wilson (British Museum Press, forthcoming). The Museum Annual Review is available from The Publications Officer, Directorate of Marketing and Public Affairs, The British Museum, Great Russell Street, London WC1B 3DG.

INDEX

The index does not include the names of contributors or Museum departments. Titles of exhibitions are given in *italics*.